WILD BUNCH WOMEN

MICHAEL RUTTER

TWODOT®

GUILFORD, CONNECTICUT
HELENA, MONTANA

AN IMPRINT OF THE GLOBE PEQUOT PRESS

A · TWODOT® · BOOK

Text design: Lisa Reneson

Library of Congress Cataloging-in-Publication Data
Rutter, Michael, 1953–
    Wild Bunch women/Michael Rutter.—1st ed.
        p. cm.
Includes bibliographical references (p.   ) and index.
ISBN 978-0-7627-2585-4
    1. Women outlaws—West (U.S.)—Biography. 2. Frontier and pioneer life—West (U.S.) 3. West (U.S.)—Biography. I. Title.

F590.5.R87 2003
364.3'082'0978—dc21   2003044826

Manufactured in the United States of America
First Edition/Fifth Printing

CONTENTS

ACKNOWLEDGMENTS

To Michael Martin Murphy, for all you've done to bring the West to light.

To Von Philips, historian, friend, for your help and comments. Thanks for the exciting times in Brown's Hole exploring long-forgotten places and fly-fishing the Green where the Wild Bunch crossed.

To Todd Smith, historian, cowboy, friend, for your insight and help on this project. Saddle up the horses and let's head to Diamond Mountain.

To Dave and Lori McGinn, friends, neighbors, fellow lovers of the Old West. Lori, you helped get this book started. Dave, let's head to the Huntington and fly-fish until our wrists are sore.

To my family, Shari, Jon-Michael, and Abbey, for your help, for the many days we've trailed the Wild Bunch.

INTRODUCTION

BUTCH CASSIDY, the Sundance Kid, Elza Lay, and Kid Curry are names well known to history. These men were some of the key members of the Western outlaw troop known as the Wild Bunch or Hole-in-the-Wall Gang, which robbed banks and trains across the American West at the turn of the twentieth century. Though their names aren't as easily recognizable, the women associated with the Wild Bunch have become legends of their own. For better or worse, their lives became entangled with the outlaws they called friends and lovers. *Wild Bunch Women* tells the story of feminine players as diverse and dynamic as the men who rode the outlaw trail.

There was the mysterious, beautiful Etta Place, a consort of Butch Cassidy first, and later a longtime companion of the Sundance Kid. Was Etta, if that was her real name, a quiet schoolteacher or an ex-prostitute seeking adventure? Whatever her background, she became a Wild Bunch fixture and accompanied Sundance and Butch on their adventures in South America.

Fanny Porter was a successful businesswoman, a madam who had the clichéd heart of gold. As well as being a trusted friend, Fanny ran the Bunch's favorite house of sin in San Antonio, Texas. Fanny's star employee, Annie Rogers, was Kid Curry's favorite soiled dove. Curry was the most savage member of the Wild Bunch and arguably one of the most dangerous gunmen in the West. Yet, he treated Annie with respect and kindness. It appears that there was a sincere affection between them. The two took long vacations together but were eventually arrested passing stolen money. The hardened Laura Bullion probably worked for Fanny Porter but later drifted to Wyoming, hanging out her shingle in the world's oldest profession. Laura became a Wild Bunch camp follower because she liked the great outdoors better than the confines of a stuffy bordello. She eventually ended up as the steady of an outlaw nicknamed the Tall Texan. Laura was a tough woman. She could ride and shoot and participated in at least one Wild Bunch robbery.

Maud Davis and Rose Morgan were two comely Mormon girls from eastern Utah. Maud married Elza Lay, while Rose married a robber and rancher named Matt Warner. Maud spent time in Robbers Roost and knew Etta Place quite well. After the birth of her first child, she wanted to settle down and pressured Elza to do likewise. Like Maud, Rose followed her husband as he rode the outlaw trail. After a number of close scrapes, never knowing if Matt would come home alive or draped over his saddle, she'd had enough. Rose loved Matt but returned to Vernal, Utah, with her baby. In desperation, she gave her husband an ultimatum—quit the bandit trail or lose her. Both women loved deeply, if unwisely. The life of an outlaw wife was far from easy and each took a number of Wild Bunch secrets to her grave.

Elizabeth Bassett was the matriarch of the famous Bassett family who lived in the region called Brown's Hole, the eastern corner of Utah and the northwestern corner of Colorado. She was a close friend of Butch Cassidy, the Sundance Kid, and Elza Lay. Many outlaws called her ranch home and looked upon Elizabeth as a big, understanding sister. She savagely fought off large cattle interests that wanted to take her land by force. When she died unexpectedly, her daughters Josie and Ann took her place. Both Josie and Ann had love affairs with members of the Wild Bunch and remained close friends of Butch Cassidy, the Sundance Kid, Elza Lay, and Matt Warner throughout their long lives.

Like the outlaws, the Wild Bunch women are cloaked in myth and legend. And like the outlaws, some Wild Bunch women went to great lengths to protect their identities with pseudonyms. This was a common practice to throw off the law and protect an individual's family from the shame of her profession. What family wanted to claim a soiled dove or an outlaw moll? This cloak of mystery had something to do with outlaw honor, but it was also pragmatic. It was prudent to mask the identity of a lady so lawmen couldn't trace the outlaw through her. Many members of the Bunch had seen firsthand how deputies and lawmen dogged Rose and Maud, as well as their relatives, trying to get their husbands.

While intrigue creates an interesting story, it also makes it difficult for historians to separate fact from fiction one hundred years later. No firsthand journals written by Wild Bunch women have been discovered. Most of the information about them is a commingled veneer of fact, legend, and myth that must be scoured carefully. The stories that emerge from the shadows are fascinating and too often overlooked.

ANNIE ROGERS

THE BEAUTY WHO TAMED THE BEAST

On a calm autumn morning in 1901, a shapely woman in an expensive dress walked into the Fourth National Bank of Nashville. She asked the teller, Mr. McHenry, if he could change a few bills. The pretty woman with rings on her fingers wanted to trade smaller notes for fifties and hundreds. She handed McHenry a brand-new bundle of bills a half-inch thick and smiled.

McHenry wondered if these notes might fit the description on the circular he had glanced at concerning a Montana robbery a few weeks back. It was a long shot, but he thought he'd better look into it. He told the woman the exchange would be no problem, but he'd have to run back to the vault, so the transaction would take a few minutes. Sure enough, the notes matched the serial numbers of the stolen money. He slipped into an office and phoned the Nashville police about his suspicions. The police, who were only a few blocks away, instructed the teller to detain the woman. McHenry went back to his sta-

1

tion and told the lady her money would be right out.

The two laughed and joked for a moment while they talked, ostensibly waiting for another clerk to bring the money from the locked vault. McHenry hoped she wouldn't get suspicious. He'd never done anything like this before. What if she had a gun? Within minutes, Nashville police detectives Marshall, Dwyer, and Dickens arrived and took the woman into custody. The three officers had just made the biggest arrest of their lives. On October 26, 1901, Annie Rogers was held as an accomplice in the Wagner, Montana, bank robbery.

Miss Rogers was a prostitute from Fanny Porter's infamous sporting house in San Antonio, Texas. Her real name was Delia Moore and she hailed from Kennedale, Texas, but like so many in her profession, she changed her name to protect her family. In addition to the name Annie Rogers, she sometimes went by Maud Williams. An intelligent saucy woman, Annie was a favorite among the Wild Bunch and a frequent traveling companion and lover of Harvey Logan, also known as the infamous Kid Curry.

As Annie Rogers and Kid Curry sadly discovered, the West had changed almost overnight. The beloved old hideouts were no longer safe. Texas, which had been a haven for Wild Bunch vacations, was now a good place to get caught. Even something as simple as changing a few stolen notes at an obscure bank proved to be a dangerous operation. No longer did lawmen have to hound an outlaw relentlessly in the field. New methods of tracking criminals and faster ways of communicating were proving highly successful, taking the fun out of good old-fashioned crime.

A photo the Wild Bunch had foolishly posed for in Fort Worth nearly proved their undoing—so would the famous photo that Kid Curry took with Annie. The modern strategy of following the hot "money trail" was also paying handsome dividends catching criminals. Not only would it allow lawmen to net Annie and Kid Curry, it would result in the capture of the Tall Texan and Laura Bullion as well.

After the Wild Bunch robbed a bank in Winnemucca, Nevada, officials discovered the gang hiding in Texas. The break came when a detective took a stroll near the red-light district and identified an outlaw from the Wild Bunch picture that was handsomely displayed in the showcase of the Swartz Photography Studio in Fort Worth. After a little detective work, lawmen were able to put faces on Butch Cassidy, the Sundance Kid, and Kid Curry—something never before done. Thousands of wanted posters with the outlaws' photos flooded the country. Further searching led to hot bills from the Nevada job. In one of the largest manhunts the West had ever seen, officials blazed the trail by tracing stolen money. The Wild Bunch barely escaped, literally going out the back door before deputies raided the apartment where they were staying. With identifying photos available and the money trail known, life became very precarious for the gang members.

Annie's jail stay was a time of personal reflection and soul searching. She knew she was no choirgirl. She had run with a rough crowd and made her living behind closed doors. Nevertheless, she had not been directly involved in this crime, although certainly Annie was an accomplice after the fact. She knew she was changing stolen money and did it willingly. It was too dangerous for Kid Curry to do it because he was easily identified, and both had felt there was little risk for Annie. It was her bad luck that she stumbled upon a conscientious teller who had read the flyer. She had done her share to help her sometime-lover, Kid Curry, spend lots of money in riotous living. Now she was in a serious jam. Officials were trying to link her directly to the robbery, and it could mean a lengthy jail sentence.

When cornered by the law, Annie, like any sensible woman, denied any knowledge of the robbery. She said she had no idea the bills had been stolen. She also denied knowing the Wild Bunch. Rather than putting her in a regular prison, the Nashville police did Annie a favor: They kept her in a large comfortable cell on the second floor of the police station. Her stay was more comfortable than she expected. In addition, a local ladies' club provided her with novels, magazines, and a deck of cards for playing solitaire. It was certainly more pleasant than the cell her soon-to-be-captured lover would have. Annie knew how to play men and was a charming addition to the police house. She was proper, coy, polite, and witty, even if she wasn't exactly cooperative. The men probably liked having her around. Officially, they kept her in-house because it was "convenient" for the detectives to question her on-site—they didn't have to travel to the prison.

Annie Rogers might have been a fallen woman, but she was likable. She wasn't the run-of-the-mill, angry bawdy girl. By today's standards, she could probably be compared to a high-priced call girl. She was able to charm the men around her and still endear herself to the old ladies who kept spoiling her with the niceties a prisoner rarely received. It helped that she was literate and articulate. When asked by one of the women if she'd like a Bible, Miss Rogers reportedly replied, "Oh, no, thank you. I've read it from cover to cover, twice." She then quoted scripture.

She pretended to cooperate with the police, who accused her of being an accomplice of the Wild Bunch, all the time proclaiming her innocence. She kept her story simple: She got the money from a man in Shreveport, Louisiana. Annie played her cards well. She was pleasant and congenial with her responses, even joking with her accusers. She won their considerations even though she kept saying she had no knowledge the bills were stolen.

Jail, even a comfortable one, gave Annie time to think. The sporting life and consorting with outlaws did not seem very appealing from behind steel bars. Annie couldn't deny her off-and-on adventures with the Kid had been a great deal of fun—

a wonderful change from her regular line of work. Curry knew how to show a girl a good time, but in the back of her mind she probably knew it was a dead end.

As time passed, the evidence against her became damaging. Kid Curry had been captured, and it soon became apparent the two were an item. Meanwhile, the police had found the picture the two had posed for in Fort Worth. It was obvious now that Annie was involved, at least after the fact.

Nevertheless, she played cat and mouse with her interrogators, flatly proclaiming her innocence. After doing more checking, the police had firm evidence with which to confront her. They could prove that she and Harvey Logan had been traveling companions. They also had witnesses at Nashville's Linck's House who would testify that she and Curry had registered on October 13, in Room Two, as Mr. and Mrs. Logan. She was caught and she knew it. When the police asked her about her family life, she clammed up. By now they knew she had worked in a San Antonio brothel and that her good friend and former madam, Fanny Porter, had sent money for her defense. Interestingly Harvey Logan, before his capture, had also sent money through Fanny to help with Annie's legal defense. While Harvey Logan, aka Kid Curry, was known as a cold-blooded sort, he treated Annie Rogers well.

She continued to proclaim her innocence about the robbery but was upfront with the police about her profession. She admitted to detectives that Annie Rogers was not her real name. Like many prostitutes, she was protecting her family with her pseudonym. She would not say any more about her past and told detectives not to probe. Annie told the police that she had been married once when she was eighteen, but her husband had been abusive and she had left him after less than two years of marriage.

Some have suggested that her relationship with Curry was one of convenience since she was a woman whose loyalties drifted toward the biggest bankroll. But it would be a mistake to assume there was no affection between these two social misfits. It's rumored that after he saw Annie for the first time, she became his favorite thereafter. They apparently hit it off from the start. Yes, she loved for money and Curry could be a savage outlaw with a hair trigger, but there was substance to their unconventional relationship, as strange and unorthodox as it was.

Both were realists and knew that life was at best a precarious game of chance for folks in their lines of work, but they lived for the moment and seemed to enjoy one another's company. Perhaps deep down Annie hoped their relationship would develop into something permanent, but she wouldn't push it and had no right to expect commitment. You didn't corral or change a man like Curry, and she was smart enough not to try. In fact, she had watched as another pretty prostitute at Fanny Porter's house set her cap for Kid Curry, the handsome gunslinger with a large mustache. This bawdy girl had staked Curry out as her personal claim, hoping he would be tempted to take her from her life of sin. She got pushy and Curry recoiled like he'd stepped on a diamondback rattler.

Annie had also seen how Will Carver, another Wild Bunch outlaw, had ended his relationship with her friend, Lillie Davis, when she got too demanding and in a sudden streak of respectability wanted to get married. Even though she was a successful prostitute, Lillie wasn't the judge of men Annie proved to be.

Lillie was a fellow Texas girl from a small town called Palestine. She decided she wanted to leave the farm to see the big city lights and have some excitement. Making her way to San Antonio, she fulfilled her dreams of living in the big city by entering the world's oldest profession. She took a job at Fanny Porter's house but tired of it quickly and wanted out. Her profession, understandably, bothered her father, and she wanted to make him proud by becoming "respectable."

Lillie had the same dream as many bawdy girls: to find a man who would rescue her from her sordid life. Lillie was always on the prowl for a client who might marry her. She got to know the Wild Bunch on a personal level and decided that Will Carver would be just the man to save her. Carver was obviously fond of Lillie since he took her on some long exciting vacations, but he was more interested in convenience and a good time than commitment. He liked having a woman about and Lillie was good company, but she wasn't the first or the last girl he would travel with.

Just like normal law-abiding people, Carver, Davis, Curry, and Rogers vacationed together. On one trip they went to the state fair, ate ice cream, and then rode the cars north for a luxurious holiday, during which they spent fistfuls of that hard-earned stolen money. Lillie kept harping on the subject of "respectability" and reportedly bullied a drunken Carver into marrying her. Well, sort of marrying her. There was probably some sort of a wedding, but it was likely all a sham. Like Carver, she'd been drinking a lot. Some accounts say it was in Texas, others say Denver, perhaps in a bar or a bawdy house. Lillie wanted a piece of paper to make it legal so she could show her parents, but if she got a license, it was bogus.

The four stayed in the finest hotels, including Brown Palace Hotel in Denver. The women were lavished with the best French fashions. The outlaws wore expensive suits (with six-guns smartly tucked into their waistbands). They drank imported wines and ate in four-star restaurants. Curiously, Annie tamed her outlaw to some degree. She had Kid Curry order some very expensive sets of silk underwear—drawers of which he was quite proud. Apparently, he was so thrilled with his new acquisitions he liked to show them off.

Reportedly, the two outlaws left the girls to pull an occasional job—no doubt needing a refill in the cash department since this long holiday was very expensive. At one time they supposedly met up with the Bunch to do some robbing. Several times they worked on their own. Depending on how long they were gone, and how much cash they had, the girls were left in nice hotels or sent back to Fanny's. When the outlaws again had fat wallets, the party continued.

Eventually Lillie's craving for respectability became too much, and Carver gave her a humorous bill of "divorcement" from their unofficial marriage. It was humorous to Carver, at least. It wasn't to Miss Davis, who soon had to go back to her job in the bawdy house. Carver bought her a train ticket back to San Antonio. He had to get back to outlawing, anyway, since he was nearly broke. He had no hard feelings, thinking they had had a good time on their vacation. Pushy though she was, he mentioned taking her on another vacation once he saved up some money, and he continued to send her gifts and money.

Lillie Davis, however, didn't take her dismissal lightly and was bitter. When law officials and Pinkerton detectives finally got around to interviewing her, Lillie Davis became one of the few confidants of the Wild Bunch who gladly rolled over on the outlaws. She told all she knew and she knew plenty. In Texas the Bunch seemed to let down their guard during their long recesses and considered her an insider. She was able to fill in the details on several Wild Bunch robberies. She verified a number of jobs and told about Wild Bunch hangouts, watering holes, and hiding places and proved to be damaging to her former clients and friends. She told the Pinkertons in 1901 that she and Carver had married at an earlier date. She further stated that she had shown her father a marriage certificate, but when the detectives looked into it, they could find no official record.

Annie did not make the same mistakes Lillie had and enjoyed her on-and-off romance for some time. Annie was one of the few stable influences in Curry's reckless, troubled young life. She calmed him and he must have loved her for it. At times, Curry could be moody and sullen, if not a bit angry, but Annie knew when to leave him alone and when to talk. When he wasn't working or partying with the Bunch, he hung out with Annie whenever he could. Besides his brothers and his friendships with Butch Cassidy and Flat Nose Curry (a good friend of Kid Curry, but no relation), she was one of the few real relationships he had.

It is rumored that at one point the prostitute and outlaw tied the knot, but this is unverifiable. They posed as man and wife under a number of names and on many occasions, but there is no record that things were ever made official. They did, however, sit for that famous picture at the shop in Fort Worth owned by John Swartz, the same man who photographed the Wild Bunch after the Winnemucca bank job. Historians are glad they did. However, from a practical outlaw-on-the-run perspective, it proved to be an unwise decision since lawmen could then track them and prove Rogers and Curry were an item.

Annie tried to be brave during her incarceration, but six

months in prison wore her down. Her lover had been captured, evidence was mounting against her, others in the robbery had been implicated, and prison life was depressing. On April 19, 1902, she went to criminal court before Judge Hart. Eyewitnesses reported that she was impeccably dressed in a black skirt, a red blouse, and a fancy hat. She put up a courageous front, but reportedly if one looked close, Annie appeared depressed and flushed, flattened by the whole affair.

While both the prosecution and defense had put on lively shows, the jury finally found her not guilty—thanks to her lover's statement. In his own way, Curry proved quite gallant, demonstrating his strong feelings for Annie. He told authorities she had not been involved in the robbery in any way. The jury believed it.

Annie wished Curry good luck and returned to her native Texas. Some accounts say she sold the big diamond Curry had given her and quit the life of a sporting woman, returning to Illinois and dropping out of recorded history. Other accounts say Annie resumed her sporting life in Texas, at least for a time. As far as we know, she never saw the Kid again, although she wrote him several long mushy letters.

Curry was captured in Knoxville, Tennessee, after he shot two lawmen. Officials discovered his identity and his other crimes caught up with him. He was given twenty years in federal prison. Desperate, he later escaped from county jail before he could be transferred to Illinois to serve his term. He fled to the West and continued his life of crime. As far as we know, he never looked up his former lover. Without Butch Cassidy orchestrating his criminal movements, the Kid's career wasn't that successful.

Near Rifle, Colorado, his luck ran out. George Kilpatrick, Charlie Howland, and Curry pulled a job. The take was small, but a posse was soon on their tail. A shoot-out occurred and supposedly more than 200 rounds were fired in the gunfight. Kid Curry took a shot through his lungs and couldn't escape. He knew he was dying by degrees so he told the others to flee while he held off the posse. Legend has it he was successful and his friends got away. Rather than be captured, he turned his well-worn Colt on himself since he had vowed never to be taken alive by the law.

FANNY PORTER AND SPORTING WOMEN

HELL'S HALF ACRE AND HOUSES OF ILL REPUTE

MOST MEMBERS OF THE WILD BUNCH had gone to Sunday school and knew about the teachings in the Good Book. They likely felt that since they were already breaking several major commandments (coveting, bearing false witness, lying, stealing, and possibly murder) in their chosen line of work, what was one more sin? Enter women of questionable virtue, aka sporting women, prostitutes, ladies of the evening, lewd women, soiled doves, bawds, bawdy girls, fallen women, dance hall girls, hookers, whores, harlots, and red-light girls.

It's difficult to discuss the history of the West without mentioning prostitution. Women were scarce and men desired female companionship. Prostitution in its various forms was commonplace. For example, more than 1,000 "working girls"

15

were rumored to have inhabited Holiday Street in Denver. Naturally, houses of prostitution were favorite hangouts for the Wild Bunch—not only for the obvious reasons, but because such establishments were often considered "safe" haunts for men on the dodge. There was an unwritten professional courtesy—an understanding—between the two groups since both parties were considered the dregs of society. They stuck together and covered for one another. The girls provided their services and tended to keep quiet about their wanted clients. In return, they were well paid. Being a prostitute or an outlaw was a lonely life. When you entered either trade, you alienated yourself from decent society, especially from family and friends. Thus, many associations, friendships, and loves were formed. Since most other social avenues were closed, they turned to each other.

As the occasion arose, the Wild Bunch sampled the wares in many houses of sin. However, if they had a choice, they felt the best houses were in the Lone Star State; in their opinion Texas had the best-looking women in the world. The Lone Star State was also a safe distance from the central and northern Rocky Mountain states, where they usually committed their crimes.

Fanny Porter's expensive bordello in San Antonio was probably their favorite recreational establishment, their "house" away from home. Fanny was not only a valued associate, she was also a personal friend. Miss Porter was a refreshingly humane madam in a business that frequently produced ruthless

and cutthroat management. She was fair to her girls and often
a best friend to them. Fanny was straightforward with her
clients and employees. It's reasonable to assume that Butch
Cassidy and the Sundance Kid appreciated these qualities.
After all, they dropped a small fortune among her collective
sheets. Fanny appears to have been a common denominator
among several women's association with the Wild Bunch.
Annie Rogers, Laura Bullion, perhaps even Etta Place, among
others, came from her house.

Many of the most successful brothels and bars in the West
minted house tokens for their customers to purchase. Fanny
issued a small token for her customers that read, appropriately,
"Good for One." The coin could be redeemed with one of the
business girls or for a certain number of drinks. Several of
Fanny's trade tokens still exist and are considered a valuable col-
lector's item. Butch and the gang probably bought pocketfuls.

Fanny liked to change the normal routine of her house to
keep her favorite clients interested in the merchandise. One
practice that she and other exclusive houses employed to show
their appreciation for their best customers was an event, for lack
of a better word, called the "sampling evening." This occasion
almost always occurred after a new batch of girls had arrived.
This was certainly a Wild Bunch favorite. On such an evening,
the house was closed except for the invited few. All the new
girls' favors were free so they could be "sampled"—but the
wine and liquor went for an outrageous $75 to $200 a bottle.

Needless to say, the house still made money on such evenings.

Fanny Porter was one of the West's more successful businesswomen. She was born Ann Porter in New Orleans in 1859 or 1860. Around 1878, she moved to Dallas to practice her trade. Being a shrewd businesswoman, she was able to claw her way to the top of her profession. While she was one of the lucky few who managed to make money and hang onto it, there was nothing glamorous about her business. Like the old cliché, she was a prostitute with a heart of gold, but she was the exception and not the rule. Working in the red-light district was a tawdry profession at best.

Incidentally, the term "red-light district" or "red-light girls" was coined in Dodge City, Kansas, during the cattle drives of the 1870s. The trainmen who carried red-glassed lanterns as part of their duties would stop for a carnal visit at one of the many houses of sin. They'd leave their famous red lanterns on the porch while they were entertained. Many times there'd be a number of lanterns lined up in front of a single door as each trainman took his turn. The term and the symbol caught on.

A discussion of this topic would be incomplete without a quick overview of the oldest profession. As mentioned, this was a cutthroat business. Few involved in this trade of flesh could afford to show any sort of charity to others. And because of the debasing nature of the profession itself, those involved were often bitter and disillusioned. Prostitution never has had a good retirement plan. The following is a short discussion on the levels of prostitution one might find during the heyday of the Wild Bunch.

The so-called "parlor house," like Fanny's establishment in San Antonio's Hell's Half Acre, was an institution at the top of the bawdy scale. (The Cheyenne Social Club in Wyoming is another famous house of this nature, catering to men with large bankrolls.) In parlor houses the girls were expensively clothed, clean, pretty, and genteel. The establishment was ornate and refined, appealing to a well-heeled clientele. Besides a fistful of dollars, a man had to meet certain standards just to walk in the door. A guest had be well dressed, bathed, and behaved. Often live music, fancy liquor, billiards, and fine meals contributed to the ambience of the establishment. The game of romance was played to perfection. Even the ostentatious bedding was changed after each customer. Sometimes these houses would be found in a town's red-light district but they could be located in higher-class sections, as well. The girls were usually between twenty and thirty years of age and charged from $20 to $75 for an adventure (at a time when $20 was a month's wages for the average working man).

Just below the parlor houses were the high-end brothels, which were often found in the red-light district. The setting wasn't as fancy as the parlor house, the girls' clothing not so expensive, but the establishment was neat. The girls would be from fifteen to thirty-five years of age. Romance was played at, but not to the same degree. A girl would be expected to spend some time with her client, however. It wasn't a volume trade. Most of these houses offered a bar and often music. The average fee might be $10 to $20. A cowboy might save up for an experience in a nicer brothel. He would not be allowed in unless he were in his best store-bought Sunday clothes, and he'd have to be on his best behavior.

Once a girl lost her looks or fell on bad luck, she might work in a common brothel in the red-light district. These had no fancy trappings or pretty furniture. Sometimes the establishment was clean and nice, especially in smaller towns. Often the rooms were dark and dingy, frequently dirty. The bedding might be changed once a day, if not once a week. Except in smaller communities where there might be a lot of local repeat business, there usually was no pretense of romance. This was a volume trade. A cowboy or a worker would come in work clothes. A prostitute in this house might entertain ten to twenty-five men an evening. During peak times (trail drives, harvests, roundups), extra girls might be hired on by the week. Some of these women were addicted to drugs or alcohol.

The red-light district also featured "crib girls," several steps lower on the social rung. These women at least had a place to sleep, in a crib-like apartment that had enough room for a bed or a cot, maybe a small stove, a steamer trunk, and perhaps a washbasin. The prostitute rented her crib for around $10 to $20 a week. If she was lucky, it might have a window. In some red-light districts there were long groups of cheaply built frame buildings holding the "cribs." In many establishments a slicker would be placed on the foot of the bed to protect the covers from muddy boots and spurs. Men would take off their hats in the presence of these ladies but not their boots. In a high-volume area, a girl might see as many as sixty to eighty men in a long evening. Many of these women were alcoholics and drug addicts.

The lowest level of prostitute was a common streetwalker. A majority of these women were addicted to drugs or drink and, sadly, suicide was common. Most would trade their services for a drink or pocket change and many were homeless, living on the streets.

Being a prostitute on any level was a profession with little hope—a dead end. It was a prison without bars—sometimes if a girl was in a better house, the prison had nicer trappings but it was just as confining. A lucky girl might marry a client or submit to being "mail ordered" to a desperate man who needed a wife/worker/slave/companion. A sporting woman could expect occasional beatings from her clients and little recourse from the police if she complained. At that time being a prostitute meant you had given up your social and civil rights. Many girls lived in fear. Harassment by the law or vigilante groups was commonplace.

Besides the possibility of violence from a client, there were unwanted pregnancy, venereal disease, and the ever-present social shame to deal with. As if life were not bleak enough, prostitutes were often abused and victimized by one of their own. Certainly pimps have an abusive reputation; however, a good number of madams in the West were also surprisingly violent. There are records of madams beating one of their girls to death. Houses of prostitution could be run like Nazi prison camps. Many girls were severely abused for minor infractions. It wasn't uncommon for a girl to be beaten nearly to death and then turned out in the street, bruised and broken with only the clothes on her back.

Even if a girl was pretty or had a good body, the profession wasn't kind. As a prostitute aged, her options decreased proportionately. High-class parlor girls in their younger years could easily end up as common streetwalkers before they cashed in their chips. This was a profession of social lepers.

It was a common practice in a house of prostitution to shut the windows, even in the summer, at least on the bottom floor. This was done to protect the house's privacy. The madam or pimp sought no unwanted, unpaid guests or interruptions. Houses were stifling during the hot months. They smelled of perfume, body sweat, tobacco smoke, and cheap whisky. Even a fancy house like Fanny's would be almost unbearable in the humidity and heat of a Texas summer.

Fanny Porter was not harsh with her girls. She loved the women who worked for her and was generally loved and respected in return. Fanny didn't mind if one of her ladies developed a relationship with a client. In fact, that girl may have had her blessings. In most houses this would be taboo and certainly the end of the girl's career at that establishment. Fanny wasn't threatened if a girl took a long vacation with a client and came back to work when the party was over or the money ran out. It seems she wanted what was best for her girls.

Madam Porter appears to have had a soft spot in her heart for the Wild Bunch. Fanny was a curvy big sister to these fun-loving naughty boys. She and her girls rolled out the red carpet when the Bunch rode into town for a carnal vacation at their favorite flesh purveyor. There was a genuine connection. The only soiled dove who ever showed ill will toward the Wild Bunch was the disillusioned Lillie Davis, who felt jilted by Will Carver. The Wild Bunch may have been a band of fun-loving bandits who paid for their carnal pleasures in stolen funds, but they usually treated the painted women in question with more respect than most bawdy-house clients—something noted by the girls.

In the late 1890s, the state of Texas was a safe hangout for the outlaws. They were careful never to commit any crimes in the Lone Star State. They bought fancy clothes and saw the sights, acting more like rich businessmen than wanted outlaws. It was said they felt so safe they frequently went without their shooting irons. It helped that the Texas press, which was mostly interested in Texas events, had shown little interest in covering their criminal exploits.

Legend has it that Fanny would only sleep on the finest, most expensive bedding. Butch knew this and often brought her fancy sheets as a token of his appreciation. On one occasion, it was reported that while Butch was in Fort Worth, he visited a linen store and bought her some expensive silk sheets. The Bunch was having an exclusive party and Kid Curry wasn't holding his liquor as well as he should. The Kid wandered into Fanny's room—perhaps for a carnal visit or perhaps by accident (Fanny rarely made house calls but it was rumored she might avail herself for a few of her special outlaw friends). The Kid was sloppy drunk and stumbled onto Fanny's bed with his boots and spurs on. He ripped up her new sheets before throwing up and passing out. Fanny was livid, so Butch promised her a new set the next time he was in Fort Worth.

There is some confusion over where Fanny Porter's house of sin was located, but most census records, arrest records, house tokens, and first-hand accounts prove it was in San Antonio. The confusion started because both San Antonio and Fort Worth have red-light districts called Hell's Half Acre. To help twist matters around more, there was also a Madam Porter in Fort Worth, but her first name happened to be Mary. She also ran a high-end brothel, and the Wild Bunch did visit it on occasion. There is some evidence that the two madams might have been professional acquaintances, if not friends.

Mary Porter was known as the Queen of the Madams in Fort Worth. She was a hardheaded businesswoman, the opposite of Fanny. While Butch and the crew patronized Mary's sporting establishment, she could not be considered the personal friend that Fanny was. However, the Wild Bunch did spend a fair amount of time in Fort Worth, taking an apartment in the Half Acre after robbing a Winnemucca bank, and spending some of their stolen loot at Mary Porter's house.

Feeling invincible and haughty, they celebrated the closing chapter of their career as the Wild Bunch in Fort Worth. The outlaws visited the John Swartz Photography Studio for what would, arguably, be the most famous outlaw portrait ever taken. They foolishly sent copies to friends and family, including a young boy Butch had befriended in Nevada. They made at least fifty copies of their portrait to keep or send. Photographer Swartz was so pleased with his work he put the photograph in his front window to promote business, having no idea who his subjects were. As luck would have it, either a Wells Fargo or Pinkerton detective recognized Will Carver. This triggered a national manhunt.

An entire book could be written about Butch and Sundance's adventures in houses of prostitution. One famous legend has Butch visiting a Chicago sporting establishment and having his heart strings tugged by one of the tainted doves. In a short time they became soul mates. The fallen maiden told the dashing outlaw how she'd come to be in such a tragic circumstance and that she'd like, God willing, to leave this path of sin, go back to the West Coast, and start all over. She wanted to go straight, get honest, find a nice guy, settle down, have kids, build a white picket fence around her cottage—and quit being a whore. Butch was touched. He bought the comely young tart a ticket to Seattle and gave her the last of his money so she could start life anew. With only a few dollars left, he couldn't afford train fare and jumped the railcars back to Utah.

There is no official record of Butch or Sundance ever returning to Fanny's after they fled to South America or of other former Wild Bunch members visiting after the gang broke up. Later, Fanny helped Annie Rogers with her legal defense after she was captured in the East.

Fanny faced some heat when the curtains dropped on the Wild Bunch—she was grilled relentlessly by detectives about her association with the boys. It didn't help that the disillusioned Miss Davis, one of her employees, rolled over on her former clients. Fanny was implicated. Eventually, she returned to the carnal love business, though her establishment never reached its previous stature.

MAUD DAVIS

LOVE AND IRRECONCILABLE DIFFERENCES

ALLEN AND MATILDA DAVIS were devoted Mormon pioneers. Just before Thanksgiving in 1874, Matilda delivered the couple's first daughter. The proud parents named their little beauty Matilda Maud, after her mother. To avoid confusion, her folks called her by her middle name. When Maud was a toddler, the young family left Summit County and settled on a fork of Ashley Creek near Maeser, Utah (which is now part of Vernal). Allen and Matilda would have thirteen children, though only five would live to adulthood.

The soil around Ashley Creek was fertile, and the family prospered until the harsh winter of 1880. There was little food left in the house by late winter, and the local stores had been sold-out for weeks. The situation became critical, so Allen, along with his brother-in-law, Joe Hardy, took the wheels off their wagons and made handcarts. Trusting in their God, they decided to make the long, dangerous journey to Green River, Wyoming, for supplies. Six-year-old Maud cried as she watched her dad and uncle ride away, fearing she wouldn't see either one again. The two men fought 15-foot-deep snowdrifts near the summit of Diamond Mountain. They also braved the swift freezing Green River near Brown's Hole. They trudged on, finally arriving at their destination, exhausted but alive. With each cart carrying plenty of provisions, the two men clawed their way through mud and over the high passes and saved their families.

The years passed and little Maud Davis grew into a handsome young woman. Firsthand accounts say she had a figure that could turn even a blind man's eye. She was a looker, but she was known as a practical girl. There was a self-assured dignity and an inherent goodness about her that made her popular with both men and women. Maud was simply a good person, kind and personable—and very determined once she made up her mind. As one observer suggested, she could have any man in the Uinta Basin—and it wasn't just because she was pretty.

Maud met Wild Bunch member Elza Lay quite by accident. Between bouts of rustling and other questionable activities, Elza was cutting hay in the meadow with Maud's brother, Albert, on a hot summer afternoon. Albert brought the good-looking young outlaw to the house for dinner. Later reminiscences suggest sparks flew from the first time their eyes met. The young man was charming with old-world manners, a rarity in the last rough-and-tumble days of the West. He was handsome and polite to a fault. Maud once told her daughter that she took one look at the strapping Elza and knew he was the man for her. She had to have him, and Maud was used to getting what she wanted.

That the young man she'd set her cap for happened to work outside the law was something the sensible but in-love Maud seemed to overlook. Times were tough in the Uinta Basin and maybe she should have wondered why the gallant Elza didn't have a real job or a visible way of supporting himself so lavishly. She didn't question where his horses or money came from, and she didn't seem bothered by the fact that his best friends, like Matt Warner, were known outlaws. Elza had worked for Matt on his horse ranch and had taken midnight rides (rustling) to fatten up their herds.

Elza had also introduced Maud to his best friend, the likable Butch Cassidy. Butch was a well-mannered young man. Both Butch and Elza had helped her father around the place when it really mattered, which spoke well of their character. Her father had commented on how they were hard workers and knew stock. Of course, they wouldn't take a penny for their efforts. People whispered that the handsome young Cassidy had been involved in the Telluride Bank robbery and there was a serious price on his head. It was rumored that Butch was more than just a rustler nowadays. Nevertheless, in that part of the West, a man was judged on how he treated folks, not what he did or didn't do in another state.

Butch Cassidy, Matt Warner, and Elza Lay were affable

men, not the hardened bad guys one often associates with the frontier. They made good impressions on the local ranchers and farmers, whom they treated respectfully. They surely didn't act like outlaws. They were amiable, hardworking cowhands who came from good homes. Seduced by shortcuts, ignoring the work ethic that had driven their parents, they had, however, made a few wrong turns and become bandits. They didn't kill people on their raids and believed that even an outlaw should never hurt or injure an innocent bystander. They were generous with their time and money and never directly committed crimes against the people in the Basin. One of the secrets of the Wild Bunch's success was that local folks gladly aided and abetted them, making it hard for law officials to capture the outlaws. Still, no matter how kind they were compared to others in their trade, they stuck large Colt .45 revolvers in people's faces and took their money.

Maud liked Butch and seemed to give him the same wide latitude she gave Elza. She ignored the rumors that both men occasionally hung around the gambling strip near Fort Duchesne or visited the saloons. She must have felt that after they were married, she could change any bad habits Elza had learned from his friends.

Maud must have met a few of Butch and Elza's other friends during their courtship. She was a girl in love, though, and probably all that really mattered was that she loved Elza and he loved her—life was going to be wonderful. She was thinking with her heart and didn't seem to worry about the future, which would take care of itself as long as she and Elza were together.

Perhaps the most troubling thing was that her young man wasn't a member of her church and had no desire to be converted to Mormonism, even though his best friends, Butch and Matt, were Mormon boys. Maud may have felt that later on she could convert her handsome fiancé to her true faith. Perhaps her personal religious beliefs had wavered as heavy doses of love flowed through her veins.

In the fall, the lovebirds were married.

Some accounts suggest they eloped or lived together before finding a preacher because Maud's parents objected to the union. Allen and Matilda Davis liked their daughter's beau— it was hard not to like Elza—but certainly her folks had objections and were understandably concerned that their spirited daughter seemed too willing to turn her back on her religious beliefs and marry a man outside her faith. It was obvious to her parents, even if it wasn't obvious to Maud, that this young man had ridden the outlaw trail and might be wanted. It was going to be difficult for their beloved daughter to have a normal life, and they warned her that there would be a price to pay for her involvement with outlaws. Nevertheless, Allen and Matilda knew their little girl. They were wise enough to know that if they didn't give her their blessings, she would marry Elza anyway and they might then lose her forever. As

Maud would sadly discover later, her parents were right to be concerned.

Maud and Elza lived together as often as his work would allow. At first, their life was an adventure. Maud was whisked from place to place by bandit friends, making sure she wasn't followed by the lawmen, so she could be with her husband. When it was certain there were no deputies on her trail, Elza would show up and take her to his hideout. It was an exciting ride for the young woman from Vernal, Utah. The spirited Maud enjoyed the cloak-and-dagger life. Sometimes her husband bought her expensive clothes and jewels. Sometimes they stayed in exclusive hotels and ate at fancy restaurants. Other times, she lived in bandit hideouts, places like Robbers Roost or Brown's Hole.

Slowly the reality of her new life settled upon her as she discovered what being married to an outlaw was all about. Her dreams of a white picket fence and that quaint little ranch they'd talked about were on hold. Elza didn't even come home every night. Being in love with a man on the run meant making concessions. It also meant constantly worrying that he might be killed or captured. As one would expect, in time being an outlaw wife became tiresome and demanding. Maud must have longed for a normal life with her man.

During one long stay at the Roost, Butch needed female company so he brought a woman friend to stay with him. The identity of this woman is a mystery, but she was probably Etta

Place or Ann Bassett. Whoever she was, Butch and his love interest shared a tent and later a cabin with Maud and Elza. There didn't seem to be any conflict among the four; they lived together happily. Maud was probably glad for the company when the men went off on their business.

At a much later date, Elza and Maud's grandson told Butch Cassidy biographer Pearl Baker that the four carved their initials into the wood on the mantel at a cabin at Robbers Roost. Certainly Maud knew all about Etta Place, but she never revealed the mysteries of Etta's life—mysteries that baffle historians to this day. Interestingly enough, she did tell her children that Etta was one of the most beautiful women she'd ever known and she liked her quite a lot. That's high praise coming from another beautiful woman. Maud and Butch's lady friend took long walks on the canyon rims together, talking and enjoying the experience. They grew quite close.

Elza missed Maud while he followed the outlaw trail, but he enjoyed the wild bandit life. After a time, Maud found herself pregnant with their first child, and she started to grow concerned about their carefree lifestyle. On August 6, 1897, she delivered their baby girl. They named her Marvel Lay.

"It's no way to bring up a child," she told her husband after a heated discussion. "It's time you left the outlaw trail and we raised our little girl in a real home." She refused to follow Elza to his various hideouts any longer. Maud hoped Marvel would be what it took to make Elza change professions and go straight. Maybe they could disappear someplace and start over.

Elza was tugged in several uncomfortable directions. He probably wanted to be with the woman and little daughter he loved, but he also loved the thrill and perks of the outlaw life and wanted to keep things as they were.

Elza committed his first major crime in 1896 and consequently went from being a happy-go-lucky rustler to a wanted criminal with a substantial price on his head. He was a key player in the Montpelier Bank robbery in Idaho. If the West hadn't known his name before, it would now. He was about to become one of the most influential criminals in the West— the quiet, intelligent lieutenant to Butch Cassidy. According to some, he was the brains behind Butch Cassidy and the secret to the Wild Bunch's success.

Along with Butch and a group soon to be called the Wild Bunch, Elza Lay helped steal $7,100 from the Montpelier Bank at Colt-point. According to Elza, the reason for the job was not selfishness; rather, it was to get money to pay for Matt Warner's legal defense. Matt had managed to get himself captured and was rotting in jail. Maybe he considered the job more as a favor to Matt than an actual crime. Maybe he didn't think about it much at all. The entire caper could have been a youthful impetuous adventure. For whatever reason, he stepped over the line. The outlaws turned the money over to Douglas Preston, a lawyer from Rock Springs, Wyoming, so he could work on Warner's defense.

Maud and Elza continued to butt heads. Neither seemed willing to give in or compromise. There were more loud discussions about Elza changing his line of work and staying home with the family who needed him. There were also a number of alarming close calls. The outlaws got bolder and more daring while the law became more persistent. The robberies had been major successes, but they also brought a great deal of pressure from deputies.

Warrants had been issued for Elza's arrest. The law knew he was married and kept a careful eye on his wife and on the Davis ranch, hoping to catch him. Several times he barely escaped the local sheriff and his men. It seems likely Sheriff Pope wasn't trying that hard—perhaps he was just going through the motions—since both Butch and Elza were his good friends, or at least had been his good friends.

The problem was Elza couldn't escape his past deeds and the law was getting closer and closer. He, as well as Butch and the Sundance Kid, could tell that the law was closing in and the old way of doing business was almost over. The Roost, the Hole-in-the-Wall area, and Brown's Hole were no longer the safe havens they had been. Trains and banks were getting organized and the Pinkertons were dogging his every step. It was only a matter of time before he was caught if he didn't retire soon.

Rendezvous with his family became more and more risky. Elza began to worry, for his own safety and that of his wife and child. Some overzealous lawman or bounty hunter might accidentally shoot Maud or Marvel trying to get him. His visits grew few and far between. Finally, Maud made it clear that her husband would have to make a choice: his family or his profession.

Elza's last job with the Wild Bunch was probably a holdup in Wilcox, Wyoming, in June of 1899. A month later he hooked up with the Black Jack Ketchum gang during a Wild Bunch hiatus. Doing two back-to-back jobs were out of character for Lay since he liked to take time and plan his capers carefully. He was probably trying to make one last big score so he could reconcile with Maud and perhaps escape somewhere and settle down. He may have finally grown weary of the outlaw trail.

The Bunch had managed to escape U.S. Marshal Joe LeFors, the famous manhunter, after their last job, but it had been close. Black Jack Ketchum had then invited Elza to ride with him for a really big score. Ketchum didn't ask Butch or Sundance since he knew they'd say no. Neither Butch nor Sundance trusted Black Jack's professional judgment. They thought his jobs were sloppy and the risk of being killed or captured was too great. Besides, he and his boys were too indiscriminate with their blazing weapons. Both Butch and Sundance tried to talk Elza out of riding with Ketchum. However, the usually cautious Lay committed the biggest error in judgment of his professional career and it cost him dearly—

jail time and the loss of any chance to reconcile with his wife.

The Ketchum gang, accompanied by Lay, robbed a train. It was a slipshod job. Almost at once, a large posse was after the bandits. At a camp on Turkey Creek, the posse overtook the outlaws and a serious gunfight ensued. The sheriff and several others were killed. The outlaws split up and a wounded Lay barely managed to escape. He was later captured in Eddy County, New Mexico, and charged with killing the sheriff, which he claimed he didn't do. He was also charged with interfering with the U.S. mail.

Lay was tried, found guilty, and given a life sentence in the Santa Fe prison. While he was in prison, Maud decided she'd had enough and divorced him, saying she was doing it for their daughter. She wanted a regular husband, a father for Marvel, and a normal marriage for herself. According to Wild Bunch memoirs, Maud was always the love of Elza's life—even if he discovered it too late. Elza loved her the way he would never love another woman. He didn't blame her for divorcing him, but it was crushing, nevertheless, for a man in prison.

Maud started over. She had a run of bad luck that she faced with a quiet dignity. In 1899, after her divorce from Elza Lay, she married a miner named Oran Curry. The couple had two children. Curry also had a son by an Indian wife that Maud accepted without prejudice (something many women would not do in that day). In the winter of 1903, Oran shot himself in his mine office with his Colt six-gun. (Some speculate he was murdered for his poker winnings, but until other evidence is found, suicide seems the most likely cause of death.)

Not quite thirty, with small children, Maud was alone and broke. Several years later, Maud married a Canadian named John McDougall. John was a sober quiet man. He was good with stock and a skilled rancher. They had a child named Ed. John loved the still-beautiful Maud and the marriage was a happy one. He was crazy about his new little boy and he accepted her other children as if they were his own. There was a mutual respect between the two, and Maud probably loved him. After they had been married for three years, John started to have back pains that were diagnosed as kidney problems. Trying to recover at Maud's parents house, the weakened John contracted influenza and died on October 15, 1906.

In 1912, Maud married a photographer named Albert Atwood. They had a child together. The newlyweds, plus children and dogs, moved to Hanna, Utah, to start life anew. Albert and Maud had a son named Albert Jr.

In 1926, her eighteen-year-old son, Ed McDougall, went to Heber, Utah, to attend school. Maud got word that her son had a severe case of pneumonia and rushed to nurse him. In spite of her best efforts, his health declined rapidly and he died. The day of her son's death, she got word that her husband was gravely ill. She rushed back to Hanna and nursed her husband, Albert, while he was dying.

Maud never married again. Like Hester Prynne in *The*

Scarlet Letter, she raised her family and spent the rest of her life helping others. She loved people and it was what she wanted to do. In the Uinta Basin, her good works are legend. As a midwife she helped bring a good number of babies into the world. Few remembered that she knew most of the Wild Bunch by name and had been married to Butch Cassidy's best friend.

Perhaps the tragedy in her life was "the price" her parents had once warned her about. Some say she wasn't wise when it came to men. To say she had a hard life would be an understatement. She lived eighty-four years, dying in 1958. No matter how much life seemed to beat her down, she never surrendered her dignity or her pride.

ROSE MORGAN

STAR-CROSSED LOVE

IT'S TEMPTING TO CHARACTERIZE Wild Bunch associates Etta Place, Laura Bullion, Annie Rogers, Fanny Porter, Mary Porter, perhaps even the Bassett sisters, as women of easy, if not questionable, virtue. Other than the Bassetts, most of these Wild Bunch women did time in various houses of sin, which were favorite recreational sites for the Wild Bunch.

Rose Morgan and Maud Davis, however, were ordinary, spunky local lasses who happened to fall for handsome, charming outlaws. They came from good homes with loving, hardworking parents. Both Rose and Maud were pretty Mormon girls who fell madly in love and were loved in return by their outlaw paramours. To use a Renaissance proverb, they loved deeply, if not wisely.

Like a character in a Shakespearian comedy, the dashing Matt Warner would make a consummate fool of himself. He'd chided his fellow outlaws for their ladyloves, arguing that a girl was an encumbrance and a waste of time. As he said in his

41

biography, "I wouldn't give a woman any serious consideration. They didn't fit into my life. It wouldn't be fair to the
girl." As far as Matt Warner was concerned, girls were to be
enjoyed, loved, and left in the dust as he rode away to rob a
bank or steal a herd of horses.

His advice is more humorous when you consider that Matt
Warner became an outlaw at an early age because of a girl in
his hometown. He thought he'd killed a romantic rival in a
fight and left his Mormon community of Levan, Utah, in the
dead of night, presuming he was wanted for murder. In his
biography he suggests that life was going well as he courted
the pretty Alice Sabey. Then a bully named Andrew
Hendricksen tried to hone in on his true love and he couldn't
have that. The fact that Andrew was a few years older than
the lovesick Warner didn't matter. He was used to making his
way in the world of men and felt he could handle anything.
One Saturday night after a church dance, the two contenders
tried to walk the comely Alice to her front porch. One could
cut the tension with the backside of a pocketknife. There was
a code in small Mormon towns—you don't fight in front of a
lady. Andrew violated the taboo when Alice wasn't looking.
He hit Matt and then tweaked his nose. When they got to
Alice's gate, the poor girl, frightened of what was about to
happen, ran to her door and slipped in. She favored Matt, but
she wasn't sure what to do.

As soon as the girl had shut the door, a serious fight erupted.

Matt was a quiet lad, soft-spoken mostly, but he had a temper when he was pushed. The fight commenced in earnest as friends shouted their respective champion on. In anger, Matt picked up a good-sized rock and bashed the bully over the head, an act that would change the course of his life. As Andrew fell to the street, the angry Matt tore up a bit of fence. Using it as a club, he proceeded to beat the downed lad.

When his temper had run its course, he heard the others shouting that he had killed Andrew. Thinking he *had* murdered the boy, he ran to his parents' house and said goodbye. He picked up his rifle and supplies, loaded up his horse, and headed north on the run. He knew if he stayed around Levan, he would be tried for murder. He was only a boy, but he was old enough to swing from a hemp rope. Without looking back, he headed for a ranch where he'd recently worked, and he swore off women forever.

Several years later he still felt he was immune to romantic attachments and had been preaching his gospel of "love and leave" to all his outlaw buddies with the vigor of an itinerate bible-thumper. His life and true home were on the outlaw trail. It was a carefree life of running from the law, drinking cowboy coffee and Old Crow whiskey, playing cards with the boys, riding fast horses—this was enough for any man. Being a bandit was his life's work, his universal calling. He didn't need a woman to fuss over him.

Things were a little hot in Brown's Hole after the Wild

Bunch had robbed a bank in Telluride, Colorado, so Matt and his brother-in-law Tom McCarty headed north to Star Valley in Wyoming to cool off over the winter. They posed as wealthy ranchers, horse buyers from "up north." They rented a place and decided to wait out the year. Their money belts were stuffed full like a Christmas goose, and they could take it easy for a long time. Matt preached on the evils of the fairer sex and romantic attachments to Tom and others who came for a visit.

They were about to be his famous last words. Enter the drop-dead beautiful Rose Morgan, a Mormon girl who lived on a ranch less than a mile away. She was pretty enough to knock the boots off any range rider. She had an enticing figure and a smile to die for. Her hair was thick and rich, and he knew he'd give everything in his money belt for just one kiss.

All his good intentions about ignoring women seemed to vanish when his eyes met the lovely Rose Morgan's. She felt it, too. The air between them was thick and heavy like the air before a July thunderstorm. The tension was palpable. His knees were weak, and all he'd ever said and preached about romance was magically forgotten in that moment. "She was a mighty good-looking blonde," Matt said in his book. "I laid my eyes on her and all my strong resolution against women oozed out of me. That girl was cut out for me and she was going to be mine."

Matt had to eat a fair amount of crow from his buddies at such a swift reversal of his theories on love and women. The dashing young outlaw, it seemed, had not only been roped, he had been hog-tied and branded after his first meeting with the lovely Miss Morgan. To make matters more interesting, this mountain girl had fallen for him. After that evening, no other man seemed to matter to her. She was going to have Matt Warner or die.

Before long, Rose knew she had this range rider corralled. She knew that when a cowboy starts polishing his boots, washing up every day, and putting on a clean shirt once or twice a week, he had serious courting on his mind. There must have been a lot of "unplanned" meetings since Rose didn't live far away.

There was a slight hitch the lovesick Matt had conveniently overlooked. He'd neglected to tell the pretty Rose about his chosen line of work. He never mentioned that he was a wanted outlaw with a rather large sum on his head, thanks to the Telluride robbery. He didn't tell her that he rustled horses and cattle. He didn't tell her he was wanted in a handful of states.

Perhaps Rose suspected that her true love was an outlaw, a wanted man. But like Maud Davis with the love of her life, Elza Lay (one of Matt's best friends), Rose ignored the signs and hoped that life would take care of itself. There's a possibility that Rose knew little about Matt's illegal activities, because he was a respected man in Wyoming and Utah, places where he and the other Wild Bunch members usually laid low and obeyed the law. Still, most of the observant folks knew he wasn't selling Bibles when he disappeared for weeks. They just didn't talk about it.

Matt didn't want to lose Rose by telling her the truth. He claims that for quite some time after they were married, Rose didn't know he was an outlaw. If this was the case, he did the pretty girl an injustice. She was blindsided by love, but she was an intelligent woman. Like her friend Maud Davis, she must have thought she could reform her man and that he'd settle down to normal life once they were married.

Matt and Rose eloped from Star Valley as soon as the snow melted on the mountain passes. Matt was anxious to get away. The melting snow meant that posses and deputies could renew their search for him and his partners. Rose's mother and step-father, Joe Romel, approved of the elopement. Rose got along fine with her family, but her folks had fallen on tough times and she would, after all, be one less mouth to feed. Besides, it appeared that the dashing rancher and probable outlaw was well heeled and could take care of their daughter. Matt was also a baptized member of her faith, even if he wasn't actively practicing his religion. Maybe he would see the proverbial light and come around.

Rose's mother knew how determined her lovely young daughter could be when her mind was made up. Her daughter was determined to marry Matt Warner and nothing would change that. Rose would soon discover that being an outlaw's wife wasn't an easy occupation.

As they rode away from Rose's parents' house, both Rose and Matt were excited to begin their new life together, even if Matt did have to do some looking over his shoulder. He still had a wad of money left from his last job and planned to show this new bride of his a great time. About 5 miles out of the Valley, Matt saw two riders coming toward them. He recognized his former brother-in-law and outlaw partner, Tom McCarty, with a rather large woman. "She was wider than a pony," Matt said. Tom was a widower (having been married to Matt's sister), and he was about to take a new wife.

The two couples got married by a justice of the peace in Idaho in a double ceremony. The woman Tom had chosen was Sary Lemberg who, fortunately, happened to be a friend and neighbor of Rose's. They got along, which was a good thing since the foursome would be rather cozy on their joint honeymoon. Sary was a cheerful sort, an expert horsewoman—if not "the best female wrangler in Wyoming," according Matt. She could throw a rope and hitch a team with the best of them.

Matt and Tom feared for their safety and decided they needed to make tracks before the law came calling. They told their wives that they were going on a camping honeymoon in the high mountains. Near Jackson, Wyoming, they camped and hunted and fished for a month. Jackson was a wild no-man's-land in those days, and the two couples were relatively safe. Matt said they "had a grand time." However, the two men were carrying a lot of money and had a desire to "spend it on their women." Eventually they headed to the mining town of Butte, Montana, where they blew their small fortune in riotous living over the summer.

Matt and Rose were desperately in love. At first it didn't bother her that there was little newlywed privacy and the quarters were cramped. At times they lived high and mighty in expensive hotels, with Matt spending hundreds, even thousands, on her. There were also fine dinners and pretty clothes. Other times they shared a canvas tent, camping under the stars, and eating ate bacon, venison, and camp bread.

As their money started to run out, Matt knew he and Tom would have to go back to work. The two outlaws sent the two women back to Star Valley for a season, lying to them about some business they had to do in Canada. The business, of course, was on the outlaw trail. So began the pattern of Rose's married life. She would meet up with Matt, and he would lavish her with gifts and fine living. When the money ran out, he would send her to a safe place and go to work. When he moved his operation to the northwest, he moved Rose to the 7 U Ranch and based his operation around it. She did her best to make the little ranch house homey and welcome the outlaws Matt brought home. When he was gone, she worried for his safety. By now she was fully aware of his occupation and was growing weary of it and the necessary lifestyle. She begged him to go straight, and he wanted to, but he felt trapped and didn't know how to quit. He told her he'd do a few more jobs and then they'd have enough money to buy a place of their own and begin new lives. Matt saved, but he also spent a great deal. He was worried about having his past catch up to him when he did go straight.

Tension mounted between them, and soon there was a baby to consider. Matt was running for his life when his daughter, Hayda, was born. He was a proud father, but he didn't stay home long enough to enjoy her. With a child in the equation, Rose became more demanding. There was more tension between them as she insisted that Matt go straight. To take the pressure off, they decided to write for Rose's sister to come for a long visit. Matt sent money for her traveling expenses. Matt didn't really like his sister-in-law, but the move appeased Rose and would give her some help with the baby. Matt always left a saddlebag of gold coins on a hook in the kitchen for household expenses. Thinking he could win his sister-in-law over, he encouraged the new arrival to help herself. He hoped that if she spent some stolen loot for things she wanted, it might keep her in check and her wagging tongue still. She was outspoken about his life of crime, and he never quite trusted her as a result.

Throughout their relationship, Matt continually tried to impress Rose. He was apparently somewhat insecure. The following story, perhaps apocryphal, illustrates this.

The winter was harsh, and the mountains of southwestern Wyoming were covered with snow.

There was only one store in Afton, Wyoming, and the man who ran it was a grouchy old miser. He decided in the late fall that he wasn't going to give anyone credit—it was cash or nothing. To make matters worse, since the passes were snowed in so early, many of the residents didn't have enough supplies laid in. The miser not only said no credit, he doubled his prices for the winter.

He had the Star Valley settlers in a corner, and he knew it. He was the only game in town. After hearing complaints about the skinflint shopkeeper, Matt decided to do something. With his true love watching, he called a large group of ranchers together, and they walked toward the general store. At gunpoint, he told the shopkeeper what he thought of his plan to cheat his customers and how the folks ought to lynch him or ride him out of town on a rail. Moreover, he told the locals to take what they needed from the store.

As they did, he had the angry shopkeeper write down what was taken and keep a running total. Matt, Colt casually pointed at the shopkeeper, said he'd pay for the supplies, but only at half of the list price, which was what they were worth. He then told the man to get a change of heart or he'd gut shoot him—that would change his "no credit" policy. As a result of this episode, the valley residents thought well of Matt and later on, when nosey deputies came poking around looking for Matt Warner, the Star Valley folks were tight-lipped.

Rose was very proud of what he had done, and he was

pleased that his actions had pleased her. He spent a great deal of money on his wife, showing her a good time. But as it turned out, what this country girl wanted wasn't expensive gifts or vacations, but a man who would be home, a man she could share a life with. It finally became too much. Rose took Hayda and left Matt. She insisted he give up the outlaw life if he wanted her back.

To make matters worse, the law finally caught up with the desperate outlaw. Matt beat the rap by hiring two very expensive lawyers who bribed two witnesses. However, it cost Matt every cent he owned. Their nest egg was gone, but he was free.

He told Rose that he'd come back to Utah and go straight if he could. Rose and his daughter joined him on Diamond Mountain. Rose was thrilled to be reunited with her husband. A time of happiness followed, but it was short-lived.

On a trip to Vernal, Rose consulted a doctor about an open sore on her leg that wasn't healing. She'd had it for years but hadn't done anything about it. The doctor told her she had bone cancer and the only way to save her life would be to remove the leg. At a hospital in Fort Duchesne, Utah, the limb was removed. Rose needed to stay in town so she could be cared for while Matt ran the ranch. He visited her often, but she didn't seem to get any better. Butch Cassidy and Elza Lay were frequent houseguests at his ranch during this time. Matt had good intentions of staying straight, but he may have wavered while Rose was convalescing in town and big medical expenses loomed. He was sick with worry over his wife. Rose didn't know that he also spent some time in Vernal drinking with his friends to numb his pain.

Things went from bad to worse. He worked on his ranch but couldn't stay out of trouble. His luck ran cold. On May 5, 1896, he was arrested and jailed for a shooting, which he claims was self-defense (and probably was). In June, Rose gave birth to a boy named Rex LeRoy Christiansen (named after Butch Cassidy, whose real name was Robert LeRoy Parker). Sadly, the baby did not live long. Then, in September, Matt and a man named William Wall were convicted of manslaughter. Matt was sentenced to the Utah State Prison.

A few days later Rose died of bone cancer.

ETTA PLACE

THE WILD BUNCH MYSTERY WOMAN

FEW WOMEN IN THE AMERICAN WEST have greater name recognition than Etta Place. Ironically, while she is the center of so much discussion, little is known about her. She is, indeed, a woman of mystery. Etta is best known as the love interest of the Sundance Kid. She was his paramour during the heyday of Wild Bunch criminal activity. In New York they posed for one of the most famous photographs in outlaw history. Later, she sailed with the Kid and Butch Cassidy for South America, where they hoped to start new lives. The gold fields, banks, and pack trains of Bolivia and Argentina were reminiscent of those found in the Old West before it got too civilized.

Etta Place visited at least one or two of the Wild Bunch strongholds, but we have no record of her participating in any of their robberies in the West. She was completely aware of what her lover did on the outlaw trail, and it didn't bother her. Later there are strong hints that she took a more active role in their informal "family" business as a valued part of the trio in

South America. She picked up a Colt .45 and became a bandit just like Butch and Sundance.

Whether she had a stomach for this sort of life can never be known (unless her long-lost journal, if it exists, is discovered). It seems she returned to the United States at least three times. She probably made at least two trips with the Sundance Kid. Most historians speculate—though it's not known for sure—that on her third trip she stayed in the United States, dropping out of recorded history.

Etta Place was a good-looking, gutsy lady with a lot of starch. She was treated as an equal by Butch and Sundance. She was reputed to be an excellent rider, as well as an excellent shot with a rifle and a passable shot with a handgun. Wild Bunch women, in general, were as bold and dynamic as the men who kept them company. A great deal has been written about her, but the real Etta was, and is, enigmatic. That's the way she wanted it—and the way Butch and Sundance wanted it. Etta Place may not have been her real name. At different times she may have gone by Ethel, Eva, or Eunice. Some have argued that the name Etta only was used after her first trip to South America—Etta is Ethel in Spanish. Another theory is that Etta was a clerical error for Ethel on her Pinkerton rap sheet and somehow the name stuck. Regardless, Etta is how she's been remembered in history.

Some Wild Bunch scholars have suggested that she acquired the name Place when she started traveling with the Kid. His mother's maiden name had been Annie Place. Her real last name might have been Ingerfield, Capel, or Thayne, among other possibilities. At the very least, it is known that she used the last name Place while on a trip to New York before she left for South America. On their journey back to the United States in 1902, she and Sundance registered as Mr. and Mrs. Harry Place. Sundance's real name was Harry Longabaugh. Few in the Wild Bunch, man or woman, used their given names, presumably so one's family could be spared the shame of being related to an outlaw . . . or worse, a fallen woman.

Was Etta a schoolteacher, a prostitute, a chambermaid—or simply a spunky woman looking for adventure? Could there have been several women sharing the same name? Concrete answers are hard to come by. Etta "sightings," like Elvis sightings, have become quite fashionable of late. An entire group of historians have honed in on her, theorizing about Etta Place as their life's work.

Etta's morals, especially for her day, were rather flexible. She may have taken care of both Sundance's and Butch's "needs," especially in South America where women were scarce. Though romantically linked to Sundance, she remained very fond of Butch for the remainder of her life. However, research indicates that Etta was a one-man woman, and while the convention of marriage wasn't important to her, she didn't consider herself a trollop.

Elza Lay's daughter, when interviewed at a later date,

suggested that it was common knowledge in her family that Etta was with Butch first and that they were a romantic couple—perhaps as early as the winter of 1897. Butch rented a cabin near Diamond Mountain in eastern Utah for Elza Lay and his new bride, Maud. Blankets were hung across the middle of the one-room structure for privacy so Butch and his companion could occupy the other side. Butch's consort in this cozy arrangement, according to some legends, was Etta Place.

Others say this mystery woman might have been none other than a young Ann Bassett, the Queen of the Rustlers, from Brown's Hole. Could Ann and Etta be the same person, as some have written? Could "Etta" have been a name for two different women with similar looks? If Ann Bassett was Butch's partner, then Butch likely went to lengths to protect her name and honor—although this cloak of confusion probably had less to do with honor and more to do with pragmatism and outlaw survival. It was good business to mask the identity of an outlaw's woman so lawmen couldn't trace her and link the two together. Both Butch and Sundance had seen how lawmen had tried to capture Elza Lay and Matt Warner using their wives.

Ann was an off-and-on girlfriend of convenience for Butch. Some feel that Ann could have changed her name to Etta and had some sordid flings with the master outlaw. The fiery Ann would have liked and appreciated the ribald life as a consort to the West's smartest bandit. While Ann was a feisty sort, she was also capable of being charming and sexy. Robbery and rustling wouldn't have bothered her—nor would "living in sin." Ann could be a naughty girl who thought only of the day's pleasures. Moral conventions for her were just that, conventions—and she hated conventions. Ann liked and understood outlaws, for she was barely housebroken herself. It wouldn't be hard to see the passionate playmate Ann shifting her romantic attentions from Butch to Sundance.

The theory that Etta Place was actually Ann Bassett gained credibility in the 1990s. Computer analysis of existing photos of Ann Bassett and Etta Place were compared, and initial tests apparently confirmed there was only a 1 in 5,000 chance that Etta and Ann were two different women. Ann and Etta shared many of the same physical characteristics, and curious similarities were spotted. A barely noticeable scar on Ann's forehead is supposed to appear on Etta in her photo as well. The scar isn't visible to the human eye but was picked up by computer analysis in a project spearheaded by Doris Burton and the Outlaw Trail Historical Association, with scanning done by the Computer Research Group at Los Alamos National Laboratories.

Some historians have tried to corroborate the photo evidence by comparing some of the dates Ann is known to have left her ranch and aligning them with the times Etta was known to be with Butch or Sundance. Most interesting is the fall of 1900 when Ann left her home for a vacation and, soon after, Etta showed up in Texas to visit Sundance. A short time later, in February of 1901, Ann again left Brown's Hole. The

Vernal Express wrote, "Miss Anne Bassett left Brown's Park on the stage for Texas."

Ann was apparently gone on this trip for quite some time. She was "traveling abroad," the same paper reported when she returned not quite two years later. According to Pinkerton records, Etta and Sundance returned to the United States in July of 1902 from South America. Before the end of the summer, the absent Ann was back at her ranch in Brown's Hole.

Many reputable scholars, however, are still not convinced that Ann was Etta Place. There is still a lot of conflicting evidence that has not been resolved. For example, on the day that Etta was supposed to dock in New York from South America, Ann was definitively seen in Colorado. Additionally, there are extant letters with postmarks to family and friends that indicate Ann's vacation was in the United States, not South America. While the photo thesis is interesting and bears more looking into, the biggest stumbling block is Ann herself. Quite a bit is known about Ann, while not much at all is known about Etta. It's easy to see Ann having a fling with an outlaw like Butch or Sundance, even a long fling. She could stay with either of the two outlaws in question for a sexual vacation, but she was too witchy and shrewish to be considered as a long-term companion. Neither Butch nor Sundance could or would have put up with her as a steady.

Frank Dimaio, a seasoned Pinkerton detective who tailed the trio across South America, felt that Etta was one of the girls from Fanny Porter's sporting house. There may have been something to this. It seems that Fanny knew Etta fairly well. Etta might have been one of Fanny's girls at one time. If so, Fanny wouldn't have minded her hooking up with one of the outlaws. Furthermore there is evidence that Etta accompanied her lover on more than one vacation to Fanny's, which suggests she knew the madam. It is possible that she was one of Fanny's friends.

There is also a credible theory that Etta wasn't a prostitute but a maid or chambermaid for Fanny at her establishment and it was there that she became acquainted with one or both of the famous outlaws. If this is the case, Etta certainly wasn't bothered by her employer's profession or the men who frequented the establishment.

Others argue that Butch might have rescued her from this location when she was only twenty years old. There is speculation that he took her back to Utah and for a while they were a couple. No matter what happened, it's plausible that she knew Fanny and stayed at her establishment more than once. Whether she approved of her lover going off to spend time with soiled doves isn't known. Whether Sundance stayed faithful to her while his outlaw friends were whooping it up with the bawdy girls isn't known either.

Dimaio thought her real name might have been Laura Etta Place and that she came from Arizona. He speculated that her father had died suddenly and she was left destitute and in desperate circumstances, ending up as a reluctant working girl in a house of sin. Dimaio believed Butch found and rescued her from that sordid life, sending her to Price, Utah, to live with a respectable Mormon family named Thayne. Here she taught school and carried on a relationship with one of the two famous Bunchers. Such a "rescue" wouldn't be out of character for Butch. He probably bailed out several girls who wanted to go home and quit the business.

Another theory has Etta working as a hooker in Fort Worth after leaving her home in the Midwest, probably Missouri. Her name was thought to be Eunice Gray. As Miss Gray she became a madam and for a long time operated a successful brothel. She lived until 1962 when she died in a hotel fire.

Richard Llewellyn, the author of *How Green Was My Valley*, felt the elusive Etta lived in Argentina, later moving to Paraguay where she married a government official. Another spin on this rumor has her hooking up with a promoter in Paraguay. She supposedly married a boxing organizer from Texas who ran a large South American ranch.

Other historians think they may have connected Etta to the Parkers in Utah. Perhaps she was actually one of Butch's (LeRoy Parker's) cousins. They wonder if she wasn't born in Kanosh, Utah, and raised near Joseph, Utah, not far from Butch's childhood home. Some speculate that she and Butch knew each other as children and became carnally reacquainted as adults.

Whoever she was, all agree Etta was attractive and could

steal a man's heart. An adjective used by those who knew her was "striking." She had wonderfully rich hair and intelligent deep-brown eyes. She had an alluring smile, a calming voice, and a pleasant personality (the exact opposite of Ann Bassett). Records indicate that she was the best-looking woman who consorted with the Bunch, and they had an eye for good-looking women. The impersonal Pinkerton file noted that Etta Place was 24 to 27; 5 feet 4 inches, maybe 5 feet 5 inches; 110 to 115 pounds; dark hair worn on the top of her head; slightly dark complexion; medium build.

At first glance, she seemed more likely to be the wife of a senator or a wealthy businessman—not the sort of woman who would fraternize with notorious outlaws. But apparently Etta craved excitement—something Butch and Sundance could give her. They had the money and the willingness to travel. She enjoyed the fast lane, as well as spending the fruit of her lover's unlawful gains on fancy settings, expensive clothes, fine wine, and expensive food. She must have completely trusted her outlaw friends—enough to uproot and take off for the wilds of South America.

Was she a lonely schoolmarm who felt trapped in her one-room classroom, as some historians have written? Was she bored with life and her profession? In an existential midlife crisis, did she hook up with two middle-aged Peter Pans and play the doting Wendy? Certainly her experience with schoolboys came in handy (her outlaw lovers often acted more like lovable, overgrown adolescents than men). Either way, she was quick-witted, educated, and refined, a woman of breeding, style, and culture. Butch and Sundance were educated and well read. They were curious and could intelligently converse on a number of varied subjects (something out of character for the typical Western outlaw).

Before leaving for South America, Etta and the Kid had a long vacation in New York. The Pinkerton detectives painstakingly pieced together the details of this trip after the fact. Butch and Sundance were smart to flee the country, because the authorities were starting to close in. Now that officials had the picture of the Wild Bunch from Fort Worth, it was only a matter of time before they were caught or killed.

Before they left the country, Butch, Sundance, and Etta covertly visited family and friends and took their big vacation to New York. They stopped to see some of Sundance's relatives in Pennsylvania. The particulars of this visit are unclear. He must have felt relatively safe at his ancestral home. It had been a long time since he'd seen his family. He proudly introduced Etta as his wife, a part she played well. The two might have left sooner than they'd planned. Some accounts say Sundance was getting nervous about detectives who might be poking about, but it apparently wasn't an extremely urgent threat.

Some argue that Butch slipped off to do one more robbery while Etta and the Kid played in New York, but this supposition doesn't square. Butch was the one who'd decided the Wild

Bunch needed to cease operations—that they'd pushed their luck as far as it could go. The Wild Bunch had barely escaped the detectives in Fort Worth. He and Sundance had saved a great deal and while he liked money, he wasn't overly greedy. Greed—a last big score—had done in too many outlaws, and Butch knew it.

Etta and Sundance went to Buffalo, New York, where the two checked into Dr. Pierce's Medical Institute at 653 Main Street. The Kid had told his family that he was going there to be treated for a leg wound that had never healed properly. Later, detectives searched the Institute and questioned employees. By that time, Butch, Sundance, and Etta had set sail. At Dr. Pierce's, detectives couldn't find any official records of their stay, but some of the staff seemed to remember treating a man who matched the outlaw's description. Perhaps the Kid had enough money to keep his treatment off the books.

Sundance might have been treated for an old leg wound, but such claims were probably a ruse. Likely, so were the claims of those who said he had lung-related problems that needed attention—perhaps a mild case of tuberculosis or a chronic sinus condition. The ailment was something the Kid would keep from his family. He was probably suffering from a venereal disease or diseases. That he had "carnal flu," as it was sometimes called, was common knowledge among his outlaw friends. He had surely taken treatment in the West for his problems, but apparently the results weren't all that satisfactory. Most agree that he, Butch, and Kid Curry had all spent at least one night too many in the company of a woman of questionable virtue. At times, any one of the outlaws was reportedly so under "the dose of town" disease, he was barely able to ride. Etta, too, surely suffered in some degree from a similar ailment. She might have been treated at the clinic, and probably was, although it wouldn't be out of character for her to stay with the Kid while he was receiving treatment.

After they left the medical institute, they went to Niagara Falls for a short holiday. Perhaps they felt they were cured. Then they hooked up with Butch and stayed at Catherine Taylor's boarding house on 12th Street. They took the best rooms; Etta and Sundance signed in as Mr. and Mrs. Harry Place. In New York, Etta went by the name of Ethel. Butch used the name of James Ryan.

On one occasion, the pair of lovebirds dropped into DeYoung's Photography Studio on Broadway in New York City to pose for their now-famous photograph. This was arguably one of the best photography studios in New York. It certainly was the most famous after their picture hit the press. Etta wore an expensive skirt, lace, and a fashionable collar. She also boasted one of the most famous pieces of jewelry to be identified in the last century. On an elaborate shopping spree, Sundance bought his ladylove an expensive gold lapel watch from the famous Tiffany's store. He reportedly paid $150 for it—a small fortune in those days. Etta might have received this watch for Valentine's Day. Sundance bought a fancy diamond stickpin for himself. Dressed up, they had their picture taken. Foolishly, the Kid sent some of the prints to friends in the West, and lawmen got ahold of them.

They had plenty of money. They ate in excellent restaurants, went to shows, shopped for clothes. Vaudeville was very big at the time, and they enjoyed the theatre. At times the two boys would visit the local bars and get a bit loose. They'd have to slip by the eagle-eyed Mrs. Taylor, who had strict standards for her tenants. Occasionally, they sent Etta shopping while they slipped out to East 14th Street to see Merry Maids, a naughty girlie show. They stayed in New York longer than they'd planned, nearly a month. A cold snap had frozen up the harbor, and they couldn't catch their boat to South America until the water thawed.

In 1903 or 1904, the Sundance Kid and Etta were supposedly spotted in Texas. Sundance is thought to have visited his sister in 1904 after the two went to the Chicago World's Fair. By late 1904, he was back in Argentina helping on his and Butch's ranch.

Etta reportedly made three round-trips from the United States to South America and back. Why she returned the last time and didn't go back is pure speculation, the subject of doctoral dissertations. Perhaps she needed serious treatment for her venereal disease. She may have been pregnant and returned to the United States to deliver the baby or have an abortion. Some wonder if her relationship with Sundance had soured. Others feel she had appendicitis and came back to the States for an operation at a Denver hospital. Some report that Sundance checked her into a hospital in Denver and walked away, never to return (which seems out of character). Some say she died before the operation (or during). Strangely, there's no record of a patient in any hospital that fits her description. Some say she died in Colorado in a shoot-out.

Around 1907, Etta slips out of Western historical legend and into Old West enigma and speculation. Butch reportedly said of this mystery woman: "Etta was a fine housekeeper, but a whore at heart."

The Wild Bunch. Left to right: Harry Longabaugh (the Sundance Kid), Will Carver, Ben Kilpatrick (the Tall Texan), Harvey Logan (Kid Curry), and Robert LeRoy Parker (Butch Cassidy). *Denver Public Library, Western History Collection, photo taken in Fort Worth, Texas*

Annie Rogers and Harvey Logan (Kid Curry) *Pinkerton Archives*

Fanny Porter *Pinkerton Archives*

Harry Longabaugh (the Sundance Kid) and Etta Place in 1901
Pinkerton Archives

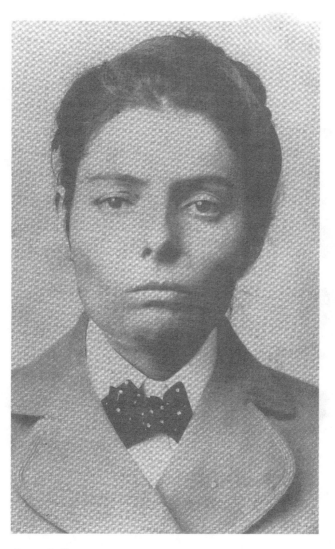

Laura Bullion *Pinkerton Archives*

Ann Bassett *Denver Public Library, Western History Collection*

This restored cabin is typical of those found in Brown's Hole at the time the Bassetts lived there. *Photo by Michael Rutter*

Josie Bassett's cabin near Jensen, Utah, lies on the edge of Dinosaur National Monument and is open to visitors. *Photo by Michael Rutter*

Elza Lay

Ann Bassett's shoes on display at John Jarvie Ranch Interpretive Center, Brown's Park, Utah *Photo by Michael Rutter*

Butch Cassidy *Wyoming State Archives*

Matt Warner, just before his death.

LAURA BULLION

THE GUM-CHEWING WILD BUNCH MOLL

NOWADAYS, ONE WOULD BE TEMPTED to call it a soap opera, even though the term didn't exist at the time it took place. The good folks of Tennessee could hardly wait for the next exciting installment to come off the press so they could read the latest news. Nothing this exciting had happened since Andy Jackson had married a woman of questionable virtue.

In the last year there had been the shooting and capture of famous outlaws: desperate men and women who had robbed banks in the West. It was even rumored those involved were the famous Wild Bunch. Was it possible that Butch Cassidy and the Sundance Kid themselves were somehow tangled up in these sordid crimes? Even more exciting was the capture of the famous gunslinger, the outlaw Kid Curry, and another desperado known as the Tall Texan, Ben Kilpatrick. If this weren't news enough, the soiled dove, Annie Rogers, was also indicted by the grand jury for her part in a robbery. On November 2, the

Nashville American had another piece of the jigsaw puzzle that interested local readership:

> Laura Bullion, the female companion of Ben Kilpatrick, the Montana train robber suspect, who was yesterday convicted of having in his possession national bank notes, was today sentenced by U.S. District Judge Adams to five years imprisonment in the federal prison at Leavenworth, Kansas.
>
> Kilpatrick yesterday received a sentence of fifteen years imprisonment in the federal prison at Jefferson City, Missouri.

A reporter who interviewed Laura before her trial suggested, "She [could] talk like a machine gun" if she wanted to. Of course, at the time the journalist recorded this, Laura had just been arrested for a serious crime and was understandably nervous. Apparently, she liked to chew gum and did so all the time, another nervous habit. One can assume she had an anxious personality, especially when she was under pressure. Others who knew her said she could be soft-spoken and calm.

Laura Bullion was probably born in Kentucky in 1873 and raised in Texas. Most think she was working in Sheridan, Wyoming, at a dance hall when she took up with the Wild Bunch. She'd been on her own since she was a girl and was hardened at an early age. Some historians argue that Laura was a Fanny Porter alumna and that she first came into contact with the Wild Bunch while working at Fanny's sporting house. There is convincing evidence that she worked for Fanny at one time, but there is nothing conclusive about her meeting the Wild Bunch in San Antonio. For whatever reasons, Laura went north.

During her time in Wyoming, she may have serviced a number of the Wild Bunch gang. Perhaps she became a Bunch camp follower. She had an adventurous spirit and liked being outdoors, away from smoky bars and the confines of a stuffy bordello. The open northern country suited her—so did roughing it while plying her trade. While she was a successful working girl, she found she liked the security of being with one man. Her first serious Wild Bunch steady was probably Will Carver, whom she may have been with as early as 1896 or 1897. Their relationship continued for some time but quickly cooled. After the Wild Bunch broke up, Carver went into business for himself. He wasn't talented at casing jobs. In Texas he was involved in a poorly planned robbery that turned sour. He eventually turned his Colt on himself rather than be taken alive.

After separating from Carver, Laura shifted her affections to Ben Kilpatrick, known as the Tall Texan. Kilpatrick became the closest thing to the true love of her life. Laura was likely taken aback by the Tall Texan's famous good looks and pleasant manner. Some say she might have known her outlaw beau as a child in Texas. At some point she became the Tall Texan's common-law wife, sharing whatever they had for a sleeping bag—striving to be true as long as it was convenient and the money held out. She is the only woman known to have actually taken part in Wild Bunch raids (Etta Place robbed with Butch and Sundance in South America, but that was after the breakup of the Bunch). Laura was a gun-toting, gum-chewing participant.

After Butch and Sundance left for South America, the various Wild Bunch members tried to carry out crimes on their own. Without Butch's careful planning and criminal mastermind, the results were predictable. In 1901, the Tall Texan participated in a robbery at Wagner, Montana. Laura came along as his Colt-toting sidekick. After a successful job, in true Wild Bunch tradition, it was customary to go on long expensive vacations to celebrate. After the caper, the couple headed east to celebrate under the names of Mr. and Mrs. Benjamin Arnold. This party, however, didn't last as long as the two had hoped. They left a careless paper trail of hot notes and were soon captured. Laura, now twenty-eight years old and feeling about sixty, faced a jail term for her part in the armed robbery.

She was sentenced to five years in prison. She maintained that she was innocent but the evidence was overwhelmingly against her. Upon release, she is supposed to have opened a boarding house. Some say she waited for her lover, but he never showed up. When the Tall Texan was released from prison in 1912, he promptly robbed a train and was shot. Laura drifted out of recorded history.

ELIZABETH BASSETT

LEADER OF THE BASSETT GANG OF BROWN'S HOLE

ELIZABETH BASSETT WAS BORN in Hot Springs, Arkansas, on August 25, 1855. Orphaned at an early age, she was brought up by her well-to-do grandfather, who raised racehorses.

From a tender age Elizabeth was a good judge of horseflesh, a skill that would become useful when she started building her own herd in the region of eastern Utah and western Colorado known as Brown's Hole. The Bassett ranch would be known for its animals, blooded horses any cowboy or outlaw would love to own. In her late teens, Elizabeth married a thirty-seven-year-old ex-schoolteacher and Civil War veteran named Herb Bassett, a gentleman she could control and who no doubt reminded her of her father or grandfather. Herb was a deeply religious man, gentle to a fault. When the family got to Brown's Hole, the first thing he did was organize a school for the valley children. He also set up a Sunday school to meet the spiritual needs of the local ranchers.

In spite of the age difference, it was a good match. Herb let Elizabeth run the ranch the way she wanted while he read books, worked in his garden, and taught school. Elizabeth was impetuous and headstrong, a dreamer, a pioneer, a doer. Nevertheless, she trusted Herb and valued him as a companion. He never had the same love of the land his spirited wife had, and he always longed for the green of his home state of Arkansas. The high plateau was always a desert to him. For the most part, their relationship was complementary—passive Herb married to determined Elizabeth, a woman who insisted on getting her way. Daughters Ann and Josie fondly reflected on their mother and father and never dwelt on any frictions between them. Both parents doted on their children and provided a secure and loving, if not unorthodox, home environment.

Both Elizabeth and Herb were extremely well read, educated, and progressive in their thinking. The pair held a number of liberal views for their day, and they passed these on to their children. The Bassetts loved the thrill of a rousing discussion. Elizabeth argued that women should have the right to vote and could not embrace the commonly accepted belief that men should rule the world. Herb agreed. Elizabeth was not bothered by traditional role stereotypes. If Herb wanted to stay home while she worried about ranch business, that was fine with her.

It is easy to see why Elizabeth Bassett and Butch Cassidy became so fond of each other. Elizabeth was a strong, intelligent woman like Butch's mother—and he liked strong independent females. Unlike many men of his age, he felt women had something important to say. He was a sensitive, intelligent scholar. Elizabeth was ten years older than Butch, and he must have viewed her as the wise big sister he never had—a woman he could talk to. The two were kindred, platonic soul mates, but she could see in the lovable, playful Butch a man hell-bent on self-destruction—if he didn't change his course. There is no evidence of any sexual energy between the two. Elizabeth was feisty and headstrong, but she was also genteel and proper—and based on all the evidence, committed to her husband.

Elizabeth had a soft spot in her heart for strays: dogs, cats, cattle, horses, and lonely men. She had a warm motherly relationship with a number of outlaws—the men who would soon be called the Wild Bunch. While Elizabeth wasn't a love interest of any member of the Bunch, she was, in every respect, a Wild Bunch woman. She had a great deal of influence on Butch Cassidy, and he probably listened to her advice, even if he didn't always take it. Elizabeth was also well liked and respected by Elza Lay and Matt Warner, among others. Indeed, she likely saw in Elza Lay the same things she saw in the young Cassidy. The Bassett ranch was a haven for these men who lived in a convoluted world of violence, lawless acts, confusion, lewd women, and gunplay. Elizabeth was the center of this haven. She was welcoming, graceful, and charming. She could make a man who'd been beat up by life or hounded by the law feel comfortable and appreciated. A man on the run or a man riding the grub line could eat and sleep at the Bassett ranch. Elizabeth would not have it any other way.

It was in the 1870s that Herb and Elizabeth Bassett made their way by covered wagon into a wild region known as Brown's Hole. They wintered with Uncle Sam Bassett until the couple could build a cabin of their own. During the winter, Elizabeth gave birth to a daughter, Ann. Elizabeth had no milk, so with the help of a Ute medicine man she hired an Indian wet nurse for her little girl. This practice continued until spring when they could procure a milking cow. The family would later tease Ann that her wild streak came from Indian milk. As their ranching concerns prospered, the couple established a warm, friendly home that was open to all.

When the Bassetts arrived at Brown's Hole, they had two loaded wagons but very little of the equipment they needed to build a home in the harsh land. They did have case after case of books, fancy silver service, china, and a pump organ. From the beginning, Elizabeth was in love with Brown's Hole and insisted that everyone call it Brown's Park (since a park was what it was and the word hole sounded vulgar, she said).

Under Elizabeth's hand, their ranch blossomed on the north side of Vermillion Creek, close to the Green River. Herb was never in good health, suffering from asthma. At one time, he also had contracted malaria, which added to his delicate constitution. He gave his wife a free hand to build "her" ranch. He stayed at home and puttered in the orchard, worked in his kitchen garden, or studied in his library. While his wife was working the range, Herb worked about the house making shelves for his books. Later, he busied himself by making furniture from rawhide and birch. Cushions for chairs were made from calf, elk, or buckskin and stuffed with hair or milkweed floss. He traded ten pounds of sugar to a Ute named Indian Mary for a white brain-tanned hide to make kitchen curtains.

Herb later became the local postmaster and moved his large literary collection to a separate building. He founded and underwrote the first public library in the region. Visitors were welcome to pull up a chair and read as long as they liked. It is reported that Butch Cassidy, who was an avid reader, spent many hours, especially on Sunday, with his nose in one of Herb's books. When chores were done, it was common knowledge that Butch could be found in the library.

During a bit of Indian trouble, Herb took his family to Green River. Elizabeth went, but she was mad about leaving. She insisted that she was not afraid of Indians and didn't see why she had to go to town. Normally, the Bassetts got along well with the Utes and were known to feed hungry Indians if they rode up to the ranch. They also traded fairly, unlike some of their neighbors. The Utes called Elizabeth "Magpie" because of her willingness to converse. Elizabeth probably wouldn't have gone to town had it not been for her children and pressure from her husband. She didn't want to leave all the work that had to be done.

Elizabeth had the ability to command an intense, filial loyalty from her ranch hands and friends. If something needed to be done, she would do it. No one on the ranch worked harder than she. According to one hand's account, she rode sidesaddle, inspecting her ranch like a queen inspects her beloved kingdom. After the start-up years were over, Elizabeth started wearing the best clothes she could afford. One cowboy recalls her riding out to see him in long trimmed dresses that flowed behind her like sails. Being a woman of Southern gentility, Elizabeth considered sidesaddle the only way for a lady to ride. Elizabeth was forever scolding her daughters for riding like men. Of course, it did little good. Elizabeth, unlike her two daughters, never wore men's clothing when she was working on the ranch. She always wore a dress, considering pants unladylike. It is reported that she never gave direct orders. Instead, she gave firm suggestions in her quaint Southern drawl. There was no mistaking, however, that her wishes were imperative commands. She simply wanted to be polite.

Elizabeth, a tough frontier woman, could out bronco, out lasso, out rustle, and out shoot most men, if the stories about her are true. Being the Southern belle she was, it's doubtful that she chewed, smoked, or drank whiskey in a tin cup, as some have suggested. She could, however, cuss a blue streak during a fit of temper.

Between jobs, Butch worked at the Bassett ranch, helping Elizabeth with range chores for room and board. As mentioned, her relationship with Cassidy was strictly proper, and he had full run of the place and was treated like a member of the family. Butch was also fond of the bumbling Herb who was quite out of his element on a working ranch. The kindly Herb could never believe that Cassidy could be capable of the lawless acts he read about in the paper. "They've got the wrong man," he said. "He never could have done this. Not him." It's practical to assume that Butch spoke to Elizabeth of his ambitions, of women, of horses, of literature. He was open with her, and she was open with him, often telling him what he may not have wanted to hear. Elizabeth didn't mince words. For her, land and family were the two things that counted in this life. She told him to settle down and raise a family. Nothing would have pleased her more than to have her young outlaw friend as a neighbor.

Elizabeth was beloved by her men. She was fair with them, but more important, she wasn't greedy or overdemanding like so many range bosses. She allowed her cowboys time to build up herds of their own if they wished. She couldn't pay a lot, but she built loyalty by letting her men share in the profits and by serving excellent food. If she went on a moonlit ride over to the Middlesex Ranch (Flying VD) or Two Bar and managed to bring back some lonely or unguarded cattle, she would give her men part of the take. If they went wild-cow hunting, her men shared part of the harvest. Two of her more famous employees, Matt Rash and Isom Dart, built up their own herds this way. After they had established places of their own, they ran their stock with hers and vice versa. She watched out for her hands, and they returned the favor by looking after her interests.

Elizabeth was a rustler of sorts, even if she wasn't doing anything more than most ranchers did in her day. The battle between the large cattle barons and the smaller ranchers was real and sometimes intense. Elizabeth would go out of her way to return one of her neighbor's animals, but she was noted for being bold about rustling from one of the cattle barons. These large concerns were trying to take her land by force, and this was one way of fighting back. For cash money, she'd occasionally drive a small herd of rustled stock to the butchers in Rock Springs or Green River. Sometimes she'd have one of her men push cattle over the mountains to the Mormon settlements or the mining camps.

On one occasion, the Flying VD accused Elizabeth of taking upwards of 500 head of cattle near Zenobia Basin. According to one legend, when she couldn't get the herd home, she drove them off the cliff to be spiteful and inflict some hurt. While she might have taken a few head now and then, it seems out of character for her to destroy a herd, even for spite.

The various stock growers associations and the large cattle barons had become powerful politically and legally, if not financially. To these feudal cattle outfits, the Hole had become a rustler's no-man's-land that was almost impossible to penetrate. Professional rustlers enjoyed a free reign as long as they didn't take the local ranchers' cattle. Instead, they brought in cattle from various large ranches in Utah, Wyoming, and Colorado.

The large outfits not only wanted the outlaw contingent in the Hole wiped out, they wanted the ranchers' land and made no bones about it. As they had done before, they would take from anyone who stood in their way. The big outfitters looked eagerly at the basin as a new piece of property to perpetuate their feudal expansion. If they could wipe out the "damned outlaws," as the settlers in Brown's Hole were called, they could step in with their strong-arm tactics and hired guns and take over the range. Yes, it was outright stealing, but they had the political clout to do it. They wanted to brand this range as their own. They didn't care that it already belonged to other families.

There had always been trouble along the eastern border of the Hole, but things heated up in the 1890s. The Middlesex Land and Cattle Company was just outside the border. Like so many cattle outfits in the West, it was owned by investors who were often from the East Coast or Europe. These investors hired managers to run the spread. The Middlesex Company hired a harsh man named Fred Fisher to manage their concern. Fisher had his eye on the Hole and announced that he was going to drive out the locals so he could have the 5 by 35 mile strip of fertile ranch land for the Flying VD.

Indeed, he announced that he might move his ranch head-
quarters to the middle of Brown's Park. Elizabeth wouldn't
take that sort of talk lying down. She rallied the locals, and
they dug in the heels of their collective boots. There were
also other threats. One was Ora Haley of the Two Bar. He
bought land near the Hole and brought in 15,000 cows. He,
too, eyed the ranches in the basin for his own needs. When
his cattle, and those belonging to the Flying VD, moved
toward this range, they began to disappear.

The Bassett ranch hands were eager to join in the fight.
They rode for the brand, as the saying goes, and cut a wide
swath for the pretty lady boss. The outlaw crowd she had so
fully befriended was an additional help, too. Cowboys, drifters,
and those on the dodge remembered anyone who said a kind
word and fed them a fine dinner. Isom Dart, the black cowboy
who was later murdered by Tom Horn, was a family intimate
who loved to play with the young Bassett children. He and
Matt Rash were principals in the group that was called the
Bassett Gang. Isom Dart had once worked at the Middlesex
ranch as a wrangler and had left with few good things to say
about the outfit. Matt Rash, who was also murdered by Tom
Horn, had been a saddlemate of Dart's. They'd brought a herd
up from Texas years earlier and had stayed because they liked
the area. Matt, too, had also worked at Middlesex and later at
the Circle K. He had little sympathy for the Middlesex outfit
or any ranching concern that tried to put the smaller ranchers

out of business. He was eager to do what he could to help the Brown's Hole locals, and that meant stealing cattle from the large outfits as often as he could. After Dart and Matt were killed by Tom Horn, four months apart, rustling dropped significantly in the area for a time.

Eventually the Middlesex ranch began to put its plan into action. When it forced the Circle K out of business, the owner, Tom Kinney, was forced to sell out at a loss. Kinney, with help from his neighbors, worked at getting even. The neighbors lightened the Middlesex cattle herds while Kinney brought in a large herd of sheep to run on—and ruin—his old range. Range maggots, as sheep were hatefully called, could eat the grass so short the land was useless for cattle. After intense rustling pressure, sheep damaging critical rangeland, several hard winters, and a drop in cattle prices, the Middlesex ranch investors called it quits. No one was sorry, and the Hole ranchers declared victory for themselves.

Elizabeth was willing to do whatever she could for her neighbors. When the local doctor died, supposedly the first natural death in the basin, the capable Mrs. Bassett took over his medical duties. She was a quick study, reading his medical books and learning the trade. She already had the practical learning that comes from patching people up. Elizabeth spent many nights ministering to the sick, only to come home and ride the range the next day without sleep. Elizabeth had the heart of Florence Nightingale, but if someone crossed her, he was an enemy for life. The Hoy outfit is a good example. They were a high and mighty family, headed by a grouchy, supposedly emasculated, patriarch who acquired the "family land" questionably, at least in Elizabeth's mind. Elizabeth wasn't above strapping on six-guns and heading off in the night to herd some Hoy cattle onto her range or burn a few Hoy barns.

One of Elizabeth's favorite hands was a cowpoke named Jack Rollas. If the famous legend is true, Jack was called out and shot by a drifting Texan and his no-account Texan sidekicks. Ironically, Elizabeth had just fed these Texas drifters lunch, having no idea what they planned to do. Supposedly, these men were finishing up their meal about the time Jack rode in. The Texans called him out, shot him, and rode like hell. With the quick help of the Bassett Gang, an enraged Elizabeth followed the killers and caught them. She brought them back to her ranch hog-tied so she could try the murderers "fairly" and officiate at their hanging. Rollas was dying from his wounds by this time, but Elizabeth handed him her Colt and told him to shoot the three Texans for what they'd done. Jack was all done in and didn't have the strength to cock the big .45, or he might have done it. She threatened to shoot the murderers herself but instead got talked into calling in the law, which was many miles away in Routt County. She thought legal entanglements and channels unnecessary but relented to keep her husband happy.

Knowing what his wife might do, Herb, who was the acting "justice of the peace," went to the barn where the prisoners were bound. He untied the Texans and told the cowboys to saddle up, ride to Hahn's Peak, and turn themselves in to the local sheriff. He didn't let them have their guns. It didn't take the Texans more than a minute to make tracks. This was a lucky break, and a man didn't get too many around Elizabeth. They thought this crazy lady was going to shoot them—and they weren't far off. Naturally, the three Texans headed north to Rock Springs with no intention of turning themselves in at Hahn's Peak. Apparently the three had been chasing Jack Rollas for two years since Rollas had killed one of the Texans' brothers in a gunfight, and they were evening up the score.

What Herb didn't know, or want to know, was his Bible-reading wife and her loyal gang reportedly followed the unarmed Texans. The Bassett Gang, with Elizabeth and her flowing riding cape at the head, caught up to the unarmed men in Irish Canyon, where they outnumbered the Texans three to one. Elizabeth officiated over the necktie party and the burial in a shallow, unmarked common grave. Legend has it she put the nooses over the condemned men herself.

According to another legend, one day Herb heard a commotion in the corral. There were a number of new cows, and they carried brands that weren't from the Bassett ranch. In the middle of this ruckus stood his wife and a few hands. Elizabeth had a hot iron in her hand. They were getting ready to doctor up the brands to make the cattle nice and legal. Herb turned around and walked away. He didn't want to know any more. Nothing his wife did surprised him.

Like their feisty mother, Elizabeth's girls were very beautiful with more than a fair streak of the wild. Even expensive finishing schools in Salt Lake and the East couldn't take the range off Herb's daughters, who, like their mother, were well educated, genteel, and properly mannered when they wanted to be. Nevertheless, they loved to raise hell and get their own way. They were born to ride and shoot and borrow cattle if the notion took them—and no mere mortal man had better get in their way or try and saddle them. Both daughters had long lines of suitors, Wild Bunch members among them, and knew how to use men. Many of Elizabeth's traits had been passed on to her girls.

One December Elizabeth started to feel ill. She was rarely sick and refused to pamper herself. She stubbornly saddled up her horse to search for her favorite milk cow during the cold weather. The next morning, she woke up with extreme stomach pains. Her daughters applied heat packs to her stomach, which gave her some relief, but didn't cure her. Before long she was dead.

One can still walk or ride about the canyons and range that were once the Bassett ranch in the northern part of Brown's Hole. It's not hard to imagine that Elizabeth's spirit still lingers in the land she loved.

ANN BASSETT

THE WOMAN WHO WOULD BE QUEEN

YOU AREN'T BORN Queen of the Rustlers . . . you have to earn the title.

Before she was called Queen Ann or Queen of the Rustlers, titles she was proud of, Ann Bassett was known as the first white girl born in Brown's Hole—a distinction she enjoyed. Her family had been among the first settlers in that desolate region of eastern Utah and western Colorado. It was a rugged land, but a land Ann grew up loving.

Ann was the younger of the Bassett sisters, daughter of the well-known Elizabeth Bassett, the pioneer-rancher who carved her own mark in Western history. During her colorful life, Ann Bassett not only made a name for herself, she was a personal friend of the West's most-wanted outlaws. As a young girl, she had a crush on Butch Cassidy, and some records indicate they may have been romantically linked once she grew up. Some have argued that she was even the mysterious Wild Bunch companion known as Etta Place. Ann was wild and reckless and would have enjoyed the carefree life of an outlaw consort.

Ann was acquainted with the moody Harvey Logan, aka the infamous Kid Curry. She surely knew Matt Warner well. By the standards of her day he was a neighbor, even though he lived over the hill on Diamond Mountain. She knew Rose Morgan, Matt's wife. She was on speaking terms with the sullen Tom McCarty, Matt's brother-in-law and a principal in the Telluride robbery. In the early days before the Wild Bunch got big, many of their crimes involved livestock, and Brown's Hole was a reasonably safe place to hide. After the Wild Bunch shifted to robbing banks, trains, and payrolls, even the Hole got a little bit too small. The outlaws would ride through and visit, but they were nervous about staying long.

Ann was about eleven or twelve when she met Butch Cassidy for the first time. As a little girl, Ann knew that her sister, Josie, had a crush on Butch, and that likely fueled Ann's enthusiasm for Butch all the more. It was noted that while Butch helped out with the chores around the Bassett ranch, he had a shameless awkward shadow and her name was Ann. She followed him everywhere and made no qualms about how she felt about him. He put up with the little girl, never guessing how pretty she'd turn out. A little later she met Elza Lay, Butch's best friend. Ann's mother, Elizabeth, was very fond of both young men. Ann had a warm spot in her heart for Elza. She may have had a short romantic fling with him when she was younger. More likely, he acted like a big brother to the ranch girl. They were oddly matched soul mates who understood each other. She remained lifelong friends with Elza.

Elza Lay, she recalled, was always interested in learning and that impressed Ann. He worked on a hay crew when he wasn't rustling, but he always had a book with him. Supposedly, he attended school with Ann one winter to further his learning. Like Butch, Elza spent a fair amount of time at the Bassett ranch. Elza fell head over heels for Maud Davis. Considering their friendship, Ann may have advised the young Romeo on how to woo the comely maid. The Sundance Kid was also supposed to have stayed at the ranch for a while. Ann surely knew Sundance well, along with other members of the gang who dropped in at the ranch for a meal.

If the story is true, after Elza had been married for a few years and was hounded by the law, he asked Ann for a special favor. He trusted her completely. He gave Ann a map of Powder Springs, where he'd hidden some of his stolen loot. If anything happened to him, Ann was supposed to go and dig it up. Elza knew the outlaw game was just about up for him—one way or another. Elza and Maud were having serious marital difficulties by this time, and for some reason he didn't want Maud to have his money. He might have been worried she'd give it to the law. Perhaps he was worried that she wouldn't be able to find it, whereas a mountain girl like Ann could. Some reports say the money was to go to his mother, while others say it was for his daughter. The important thing is he trusted his old friend, Ann.

Butch, Elza, and the Sundance Kid were very grateful to the Bassett family and some of the other Brown's Hole folk, according to Ann's autobiographic account. She had a tendency to tell some tall tales, and one has to take her narratives with a chunk of salt. According to her, to show their appreciation, the outlaws put on what has been called in legend the Outlaws Thanksgiving Day Feast. In her memoirs, Ann says this holiday was not soon forgotten among the locals. She recalls what the outlaws wore:

> Dark suits with white shirts (vests were worn), stiff collars and bow ties to serve in. No man would be seen minus a coat and bow tie at the party. Mustaches must be waxed and curled. The women wore tight fitted long dresses with leg-o-mutton sleeves and boned collars—hair done on top of the head either in a French twist or a bun and bangs curled. Girls in their teens wore dresses three inches below their knees.

At the feast, the Brown's Hole folks ate:

> Blue point cocktails, roast turkey with chestnut dressing, giblet gravy, cranberries, mashed potatoes, candied sweet potatoes, creamed peas, celery, olives, pickled walnuts, sweet pickles, fresh tomatoes on crisp lettuce, hot rolls and sweet butter, coffee, whipped cream, Roquefort dressing, pumpkin pie, plum pudding, brandy sauce, mints, salted nuts.

Ann commented that Butch and his crew were better as gunmen than as waiters. She and Josie teased Butch all evening about how he was dressed. She claims in her memoirs that this feast took place in 1895. Her memory for fashions and food was probably accurate, but the year doesn't seem right. Butch was behind bars in Wyoming during the fall of 1895. Ann might have made the whole thing up or gotten her dates wrong. Maybe she built the event on a partial dinner or dinners the outlaws cooked for their friends and got mixed up on the details. Perhaps when she composed her memoirs, she did some creative writing (based on some fact, of course), dropping in the famous outlaw names to make her narrative more exciting. True or not, the story only adds to the legend and mystique of the Wild Bunch and their women.

After Ann started to blossom, a neighbor said he saw Ann and Josie get into a serious fight. The observer says they argued over one of the outlaws' affections. It was apparently a "knock-down-drag-out" affair. There was punching, screaming, kicking, and hair pulling. Butch was supposed to have been the cause of the fight, but this could be another of those outlaw-promoting rumors that circulated with regularity throughout the area. The sisters fought a lot as they were growing up. A fight of this nature wouldn't be out of character since they were both known to punch, kick, bite, and scream—especially at each other. As her sister's romance with Butch cooled, Ann hints that hers heated up. Again it's dangerous to take Ann completely at her word since she's prone to creative fabrication. Still, considering her personality, it's not hard to believe she made some sort of a love nest with Butch and/or

Sundance at a secret hideout, warming up the cold nights. In spite of the sisterly spats that sometimes drew blood, Ann and Josie remained quite close throughout their lives.

Ann, like her mother and sister, loved the landscape of eastern Utah and western Colorado. The Bassett women were viscerally connected to the valleys, basins, and mountains of the region. While her sister, Josie, didn't mind household chores, Ann hated such activities (there was little domestic about her). She longed to be on horseback, riding the range. She liked to oversee and direct. While her mother and sister were never afraid of getting out of the saddle, digging holes, branding calves, or mending fences, Ann never enjoyed such labors— they'd mess up her carefully choreographed wardrobe. Although not the hard physical worker that her mother and sister were, Ann was, nevertheless, keenly interested in ranch life and furthering her concerns. She wanted the rewards without the sweat. Josie once commented that Ann got bored easily, and "couldn't be satisfied if it was a long ride to town." Ann liked an audience and putting on a show for anyone who would watch. Underneath her confident exterior was an insecure woman who, as Shakespeare said, "slenderly knew herself."

Ann was a tomboy without dirt under her nails. She was self centered and wanted to be in the middle of things, the opposite of Josie. She could be as determined and vindictive as a cornered prairie rattler. Nevertheless, like all Bassetts, she was also kind and giving to those who were down-and-out.

Elizabeth was able to keep her reined in; however, after her death, Ann ran unchecked. Normally, Josie would have stepped in and tried to mother Ann, but she had problems of her own—an unplanned baby and wedding preparations. Josie was out of the house before the shock of Elizabeth's death had faded. Their father, Herb, was a pushover. Ann loved him dearly, but she disregarded his wishes.

Herb was well-mannered but weak, and he could not control his strong-willed daughter. Ann was well read and educated for her day, as all the Bassetts were, but she was reportedly a below average student. In fact, she was an academic handful. The poor nuns at St. Mary's, after a hellish year, kindly asked Herb to never, never, never send her back. One can only imagine the stunts she pulled and the rules she broke. The gentle Herb was committed to her education, however. He sent her to other schools back east. She says in her memoirs she went to an exclusive finishing school in Boston, but this might have been a fish story. For a time, her western neighbors were fooled by her highfalutin façade. She enjoyed the notoriety she created for herself. Beyond the makeup (it was rumored she blatantly painted her cheeks red as bawdy girls did) and an affected East Coast accent she'd carefully cultivated, she was still a Western girl who couldn't get the red rock canyons out of her blood.

As a thirteen-year-old girl, Ann made up her mind to rope a silvertip grizzly cub. In her day, grizzlies still roamed the

Hole with some frequency. She couldn't have been naive about the dangers. She was simply stubborn. The bratty girl did what she wanted without worrying about the consequences. After Ann roped the baby bear, the mother bear decided to rip Ann into 112 pieces. The foolish, but lucky, girl managed to slide up a tree just in time to avoid attack. The enraged bear shook the aspen desperately, hoping to loosen the girl clinging to the leafy branches. When that didn't work, the sow supposedly took her anger out on Ann's horse. The commotion caught the attention of some Bassett ranch hands. They ventilated the bear with their rifles and rescued the girl. She had no regrets.

Ann was the only Bassett child her father, the passive Herb, ever physically disciplined. He whipped her in a rare fit of anger. Herb had told young Ann not to play with an ax. He'd been barking some cottonwood logs and was taking a break. She told him no; she wanted to peep the logs, too, just like a man did. This was a dangerous job, as many a man missing a foot could testify. A child who didn't know what she was doing could get herself seriously hurt. He told her again to stop, and she had a tantrum and called him a "stupid son of a bitch" and told him to leave her alone. This resulted in the famous trip to the woodshed, the first and only time Herb Bassett used corporal punishment on a child. This was quite a step for her father, who didn't believe in spanking. However, for the most part, Ann knew how to completely manipulate her father, and since her mother died when she was young, she had little parental influence to guide her.

None of the iconoclastic Bassett females would or could be tamed by men, society, or social conventions. Each marched to her own drummer. Grace McClure puts it best in her book, *The Bassett Women:* ". . . the intensity of her [Ann's] emotions and the strength of her will made it unthinkable that she could have denied herself . . . satisfaction when she was ready for it. No moral consideration, no fear of gossiping tongues, not even the larger fear of pregnancy could have prevented it. She was and always will be this way . . . not counting the costs." Thinking about long-term ramifications, cause and effect, or the results of one's actions wasn't a Bassett characteristic. Ann was an impulsive, epicurean actor on life's proverbial stage, doing what felt good at the moment, never looking beyond the present.

Ann knew men were attracted to her and was keenly aware of her charms. She flirted, teased, and manipulated shamelessly to get her way or show off. Ann knew that many women looked down on her, but that didn't matter. McClure suggests that Ann considered men objects to be used—and use them she did (for pleasure, for power, for courting sympathy, for getting something done she didn't want to do herself, for any purpose that suited her). Ann Bassett was a brilliant opportunist.

When the large outfits tried to push the small ranchers out of Brown's Hole, Ann stepped into her mother's place as the

vanguard for the underdogs. She lashed out with blind reck-
lessness, fighting with all her soul, using every trick she knew.
Another full-scale range war was developing, and Ann was
caught in the middle—or more accurately, she willingly
placed herself in the middle. Like her mother, she was the
spokesperson and rallying point for the loyal opposition. Ann
and her comrades became more than a thorn in the sides of
the large cattle concerns. With Elizabeth gone, the barons
thought that with a little force, they could push the ranchers
out of the basin and divide up the fertile grazing land and
water rights among themselves. They had not counted on
such obstinacy from the local ranchers, the cost in hard cash,
the lost man hours, and the number of cattle lost to rustlers,
even after Elizabeth's death. Predictably, no ranch was harder
hit by the locals than the Two Bar, the ranch Elizabeth had
hated the most.

Desperate, the powerful cattleman's association turned to
drastic measures. They collected money from each of their
members and established a war fund, hiring armed riders to
strengthen up their lines—heaven help the innocent rancher
who got caught in the wrong place at the wrong time. They
applied pressure on political officials to further their interests,
including well-placed bribes. They discovered they could
bring offenders to trial, but the juries, which were made up of
small-scale ranchers and cattlemen, were not sympathetic to
their cause and acquitted the offenders with a slap on the

wrist. Since the legal system didn't work and they couldn't buy the results they wanted, the only choice was to take the law into their own hands. They hired range detectives like Tom Horn who "had a system that never failed."

Horn didn't come cheap, though. After expenses, he was paid at least $500 a head. Tom Horn was a proven killer, but there was a moral code to his transactions he always followed. He had to personally catch the rustler in the act of stealing before he employed his system that didn't fail. With his trusty .30-.30 rifle the results were permanent. Going undercover into the Hole as a cowboy named Hicks, Tom Horn found the evidence he needed.

After Elizabeth died, two of her so-called "Bassett Gang" members helped at the Bassett ranch while they built ranches of their own. These two family friends were Matt Rash and Isom Dart. Matt was especially helpful. Toward the end of the nineteenth century, Matt and Ann possibly became engaged. During one fateful summer, some reports even have Rash building a new, bigger cabin for his upcoming nuptials. To free up his time, Matt Rash hired Hicks to work his cattle. Over the summer Hicks saw both Rash and Dart commit the crimes he'd been sent to stop. He left them each a note telling them they had a week to leave the country or they'd be killed. Neither man left, blowing off the threat. Tom Horn stalked each man and shot him in cold blood.

These deaths naturally sent a shock wave through the

region. Ann herself possibly received a warning letter too. However, in that day, killing a woman for any reason would have been completely unacceptable—even if the woman was a rustler and guilty. Even Tom Horn wouldn't shoot a lady. The letter to Ann, if it really was sent, was only a scare tactic.

Ann spoke at the funerals of Rash and Dart, and by then the Brown's Hole residents had learned that Hicks was really Tom Horn. She cursed the killer and the ranchers who had paid him.

Were Matt Rash and Ann Bassett really engaged? Or was this a clever invention by opportunistic Ann to generate sympathy for her cause and cast aspersions on the godless enemy? Several Western scholars have wondered. The two obviously knew each other quite well. He was a family friend, and Ann must have known him from the time she was a young girl. They might have been lovers; in fact, knowing Ann, they probably were. But there has been question about how formal their engagement was. Ann claimed a part of Rash's estate after he was murdered and finally received a modest, almost token, cash settlement. Matt's father fought her claim, saying he knew nothing about any relationship she'd had with his son. Nevertheless, politically, an engagement, fake or not, was an excellent move on her part to generate sympathy for the cause as the bereaved woman, the woman of the man who was murdered by the ruthless cattle lords and the killer Tom Horn. If nothing else, Ann knew how to play to her public.

Rustling losses slowed down after Rash and Dart were killed but soon picked up again. Ann and company took from the big ranches whenever they could, especially from the hated Two Bar, her main target. She and her men patrolled the borders of their rangeland relentlessly. They reportedly shot any cattle that wandered onto their land and, according to some Bassett legends, even ran herds over steep cliffs so they'd fall to their deaths. Her mother had been accused of the same mischief. If any wholesale destruction occurred, Ann would have been more likely to commit it than her mother. However, it's more likely that Ann found some way to rid the large ranchers of cows without killing off herds. Ann may have killed a few cows to make a point (specifically Two Bar animals) once or twice, but there is no solid proof that she destroyed whole herds.

When Ann was twenty-six years old, she came up with a scheme to really get back at the Two Bar. She knew that Hi Bernard, the manager, was one of the keys to the large ranch's success. Ann was able to seduce him with little effort. Though he was old enough to be her father, the sultry Ann plucked him like a Mexican guitar string. In 1904, the smiling Hi became Ann Bassett's first husband. Not only did she plan to hurt the Two Bar efforts by this move, she felt that Hi could work to benefit her ranch. As soon as Hi married Ann, no matter that he was the best manager in the region, he was promptly fired from the Two Bar.

Hi soon discovered that he had married a woman who was part goddess, part gut-shot grizzly bear. Ann was a beauty and Hi liked to be seen with her, but she was also temperamental and prone to fits of childish anger. Josie's backhanded comment about the marriage was, "He [Hi] was in his second childhood." Hi helped Ann get more land and build up her ranch, but soon things started to sour. Not only did Ann have too much fire for the older man, he quickly discovered that she was much prettier outside than inside and that she was as faithful as an alley cat.

They managed to stay married for six long rocky years, although during the last few years, Hi was understandably gone from the ranch most of the time. Ann won most of the verbal battles against the soft-spoken man, although one time he got back at her and she never forgave him. Hi managed to belittle and embarrass her in front of their neighbors and ranch hands, something Ann couldn't bear.

It was a matter of pride for a cowboy to take any horse he had drawn in the remuda and ride it for that day's work. On the morning in question, a cowboy drew a rough-broken horse that wouldn't stop bucking. Apparently, each time this frisky bronc bucked, it broke a great deal of wind. This process went on for some time while the determined cowboy stuck with the bucking mount for all he was worth. Ann was a little disgruntled by how long it took since she wanted to get on with the roundup and branding. She was annoyed with the cowhand for not mastering this mustang more quickly. Ann prided herself on being a wonderful horsewoman who could ride as well as a man. Standing next to Hi and a group of neighbors and cowboys, she said boldly, "I can do a lot better than that."

The normally quiet Hi said in a loud voice, "Yes, God-damnit, I've heard you fart louder than that horse lots of times."

Appearances and propriety, which were so important to Ann, had been violated. Hi had overstepped the line for the last time. But in his own way, he'd gotten back at the woman who'd made his life difficult in a unique way. Hi wasn't surprised when he found a young rider named Yarberry spending time with Ann when he returned from his next trip to Denver.

In the last year of her marriage, Ann was caught red-handed by a range detective rustling Two Bar beef. One carcass was flagrantly hanging, partly butchered, in the barn. The hide (with brand) and guts were not far off beside the road. Her latest revenge on the Two Bar, besides taking the beef in question, had been closing off the Douglas Mountain water hole. Things were tense because the larger ranch needed Ann's water to expand. The Two Bar, with the hide as evidence, pushed to bring her to justice. Their case was a little shaky, and even the range detective thought they should wait for more proof, but the manager was getting desperate about the water issue. If they could convict Ann, they could easily get what they needed.

The Two Bar, it seems, wasn't popular with the locals, and neither was its manager, Bill Patton (Hi's replacement). Ann was viewed as the underdog. For the folks in that region, this was the trial of the century. They got together and rented the local opera hall in Craig, Colorado, so there'd be enough room for the observers. It was the big mean rancher versus the flamboyant Ann, the little girl who was trying to save her ancestral home.

During the trial a reporter got pushy. Normally, Ann was good with the press and wanted them on her side, but she must have been tired. She got curt with the man and he tried to get back at her by calling her "Queen of the Rustlers" or "Queen Ann" in his copy. The name stuck. From then on she was often referred to by one of these two titles. Both pleased her immensely. The angry reporter, who was trying to blast her in print, had done her a favor.

Queen Ann graced the opera room for her day in court. She boasted a perfect figure. Her thick dark hair was perfectly combed, and her expensive East Coast clothing was the talk of the town. She pranced into the theater like royalty. This was her moment and she relished it. The first trial resulted in a hung jury—ten wanted to let her off, two felt she was guilty. One of the men who voted to let her go said, "We thought she probably did take the beef, but the court sure didn't prove it." It didn't hurt that most of the men on the jury didn't like the way the Two Bar was honing in on Douglas Mountain water and had at one time or other taken a few beef cows themselves.

The Two Bar tried again. The lawyers were costing a lot, but Ann enjoyed the notoriety. In the next trial, the Two Bar owner, Ora Ben Haley, got caught in an elaborate lie about his taxes and the number of cattle he owned. This seriously hurt his case since he ended up looking like a fool—as well as a land-hungry feudal lord. It also didn't help the Two Bar cause that Bill Patton, the ranch manager, had inadvertently tangled with a lawman in Baggs, Wyoming, and gotten himself shot to death. After a day of deliberation, the jury acquitted Ann. For years her family had battled with the Two Bar; now Ann had beat Haley in court and it felt good.

When Ann was in her thirties, she found true love with a man named Frank Willis. They married in 1923. He was one of the few men who wasn't bothered by her moods, her temper, or her fickle ways. Josie said to him, "The devil has it in for you, Frank, and is paying you back in wives." Frank was a miner so they traveled a lot, which was good for Ann—she didn't get bored. They never had children. At one time, Frank worked for Elza Lay when times were hard for the Willis family. Elza had never forgotten Ann's kindness or their friendship. Ann also saw her old friend Butch a number of times. They reminisced about the good old days when the West was wild and they were young. One time they met on a mining site in Nevada. They used assumed names, and she never spoke of their meetings with an outsider until the 1930s.

Ann never lost her feistiness. In Boron, California, in the late 1930s, a circus bear turned mean and escaped into the mountains after a train derailment. At age sixty, Ann ripped down the reward poster, which read BEAR WANTED DEAD OR ALIVE, loaded up her Winchester rifle, and trailed the animal in the hills for several days. She shot the bear and got her reward. The 1950s found Ann and Frank in Utah prospecting for uranium and spending summers in Brown's Hole. Ann died in May of 1956 at the age of seventy-eight, never having lost her love for the red rocks, flowing water, and lush green grass found in the region of her childhood home.

JOSIE BASSETT

NEVER TAMED OR BROKEN

As a young girl, Josie Bassett followed two wagons as they rolled into the wilderness that had been named Brown's Hole by mountain men. She spent her first Brown's Hole winter in her uncle's small cabin until her family could build a place of their own. Her mother, Elizabeth, had fallen in love with this haunting basin, the steep red rock cliffs, the forested mesas, and the rich prairie grass that had until recently belonged to the buffalo. Elizabeth was determined to carve out a home and ranch to be proud of—even if her husband didn't share her passion or her love of this untamed land.

Josie remembered being keenly aware that her uncle's cabin didn't have windows and this bothered her. Like her mother, Josie, too, loved this fertile piece of the Colorado Plateau and never wanted to be far from it. In this land, the threat of an Indian attack was constant. She remembers being packed up and taken to town, kicking and screaming, worrying that their ranch might be burned when they returned. She was on a horse from the time she could walk and was shooting a rifle as soon as she could hold it steady. Before she was twelve, she could skin a deer or mend a corral.

Josie Bassett was born in 1874, and when she was young, the West was wild and woolly. The open range stretched ahead for days without a fence in sight. Men on the dodge were frequent guests at her home, treated with respect as long as they behaved. When she was fifteen, she met one of the most famous outlaws of his era, Butch Cassidy, who spent the winter at her home. She no doubt traced the careers of the Wild Bunch members via exaggerated newspaper articles. It must have amused her that most of the Wild Bunch, including the Sundance Kid, had spent countless nights at her home and eaten many a meal at the Bassett table. She must have laughed at the outrageous yarns that were spun about her old friends.

Josie not only lived long enough to see the rise and fall of the Wild Bunch, she saw the world grow up. She lived long enough to see penicillin, the jet age, two world wars, and the horrific destruction of nuclear weapons. Nevertheless, she chose to spend her life living the way she always had, close to the land and on her terms.

As children, she and her sister, Ann, were a handful. The West never bred a more colorful or gorgeous pair of sisters. It would be an understatement to say they had the men of Brown's Hole and western Colorado wrapped about their little fingers. Each had a temper, Ann's being more mercurial. At the same time, both girls could be kind and downright generous, as well as charming and seductive. Both were manipulative, although Ann was worse. These two had the innocence of a schoolgirl blended with a streetwalker's savvy.

In today's parlance, Josie "got around." She was married five times and had a string of lovers. She fit the profile of the current sexual revolution more completely than the closing days of Victorianism allowed. She was a tarnished scandalous woman. Like her sister, Josie was often the butt of country gossip, a scarlet woman. Neither St. Mary's School in Salt Lake nor Miss Potter's School for Girls in Boston could break her spirit. One can almost see either Bassett sister in a fancy dorm, trying to rustle a game of five card stud, telling dirty jokes in Latin while conjugating French verbs for the next day's lesson, perhaps rolling a cowboy cigarette and letting it hang from her lips to shock her blue-blooded roommates.

Butch Cassidy came to the Bassett ranch to escape from a posse in 1889. He was keeping a low profile after committing a robbery in Colorado. He was a good-looking, likable young outlaw, the kind of man who could take a young woman's heart without meaning to. He caught Josie's eye in an instant. Josie was in full bloom at the time and would certainly have attracted the eye of the young outlaw. At this time she often referred to him as her "Brown's Park beau." Butch took her to dances and if legend is fact, they soon became an item, dating and enjoying each other's company.

Butch spent a lot of time reading in Herb Bassett's library. Since Josie had been well educated and had been off to school, a man who was strong and bold, yet sensitive enough to read good literature, was surely an attractive fellow. He could handle himself in a gunfight or fistfight, he could rustle and brand a stolen steer with ease, he could ride a wild mustang, but he could also talk with authority about the Lake Poets and had read Scott, Tennyson, and Austen.

Josie recalled her first meeting with Cassidy. There had been a horse race at the Crouse ranch on the north side of the Green River. It was a long straight track, unlike the oval ones popular today. The horses were raced to one end where they turned around, which was precarious, and spurred back to the finishing line. It was an exciting event. Folks from all over Brown's Hole came to see the fun, bringing a picnic. Whiskey flowed and later there was a barn dance.

Butch, who was known as George Cassidy in those days, rode one of Crouse's favorite horses. "I thought he was the most dashing and handsome man I ever seen," Josie wrote. "I was such a young thing . . . and looked upon Butch as my knight in shining armor. He was more interested in his horse than he was in me, and I remember being very put off by that. I went home after being snubbed by him and stamped my foot in frustration."

Josie admits in her account that Butch and she were later lovers. Apparently, one time some men were after Butch and he hid in the Bassett barn. He read books from the library, but he wasn't allowed to read by lantern at night because of the fire danger. He told Josie he'd be bored up there all by himself. Josie adds, "Well, all I can say is, I didn't let him get bored."

The love affair may have been rekindled off and on as a romance of convenience. Butch was gone a good bit of the time, and Josie wasn't one to sit home alone. She apparently sparked Butch between jobs. There is some evidence that they rendezvoused at towns in Nevada and Wyoming for a weekend, but this is undocumented. Butch and Josie remained good friends. Josie claims she saw Butch as late as the 1920s and that her sister, Ann, had seen him from time to time, too.

Josie also spent time with family friend Elza Lay in the early 1890s. He worked for the Bassetts off and on, staying at least one winter with the family. Josie always referred to Elza as "the finest gentleman I've ever known." He may have courted both sisters. He did spend some time with Ann, although Ann said she and Elza were never serious. Elza and Josie went to dances together and spent a lot of evenings talking. They enjoyed conversing with each other. Elza's grandson suggested that Elza and Josie were lovers at one time— although Lay family memoirs suggest they must have had an understanding and they might not have been passionate. They were certainly fond of each other but Elza was a wanted outlaw, and Josie was looking for a man she could keep by her side full-time.

Sadly, she was never able to find the romantic relationship she desired. Josie would go through five husbands, divorcing four of them.

Her promiscuous behavior caught up with her sooner than she had hoped. She had been a little too close with the good-looking Jim McKnight, a ranch foreman her mother had hired before she died. McKnight became Josie's first husband, and it wasn't a good match. She was quite pregnant when she said, "I do." When her mother died, Josie was several months along. The union brought the couple two children. They fought a great deal, and after a few years called it quits. However, they managed to stay friends after the divorce. Josie tended to be a lot more domestic than her sister. She actually liked the duties involved in being a ranch wife, and she enjoyed her children. She was fond of taking care of a kitchen garden, making soap, baking bread and cookies, keeping house, and helping with ranch chores. Had Josie been a better judge of men, she could have been quite content as a rancher's wife. As it was, she had bad luck with men.

She was widowed once. There were rumors that she'd poisoned the man, adding to her local mystique. She had been heard to say "if you can't get rid of a man one way, you get rid of him another." But she didn't poison Nig Wells. She rather enjoyed him, but Nig at times was a serious drinker, something she had little tolerance for. Nig and Josie were well matched, except for this issue. Most of the time Nig was a good rancher who worked hard and was nice to her kids. Occasionally, however, he went on a drinking binge, which caused tension.

To put an end to his drinking problem, Josie ordered a product called The Keen Cure from a Salt Lake City pharmaceutical company. It was supposed to cure alcohol- and drug-related problems. All you did was put a few spoonfuls in your coffee and after a few days, if the ad didn't lie, you were cured. Nig was going on a bender for the New Year's holiday, so Josie thought it was a perfect time to try her curing powder. Apparently, The Keen Cure didn't work like she'd hoped. Nig stumbled home after a drinking binge looking pale. He said he didn't feel well. He threw up, went to bed, and died. Rumors aside, poison was not her style. Josie was passionate when angry, but her anger blew over quickly. She might shoot a man or stab him in a fit of anger, but she'd never poison him by degrees. Furthermore, she liked Nig.

Because of the gossip and ensuing news reports, Josie was hauled in for official questioning. She wasn't amused. She obeyed the official summons, but she came prepared. Josie angrily strapped a Colt six-gun about her waist and carried her deer rifle. She wasn't going to be trifled with over some gossip. Not surprisingly, the case was closed. Another rumor suggested Josie had shot her first husband during a tantrum; however, no bullet wounds were found in the estranged Jim McKnight.

With Nig gone, Josie could no longer stay at Brown's Hole.

She was just about broke. Some Ute land had opened up for homesteads, and she took advantage of it. She settled in a lovely canyon beyond the Green River on a place called Cub Creek and lived with a man named Ben Morris, who had helped out on her ranch after Nig died. The two were unsuited for each other. Ben was a passable hand but a slob. In Utah, she married Ben to placate her daughter-in-law and to keep the morally strict Mormon community from looking down on her. Tension between them mounted. One day Ben complained about some lumps in the gravy. Josie had been in the field all day clearing brush and was tired. She threw the gravy on Ben and told him to wear it. Ben knew that Josie was serious this time. He said, "She gave me fifteen minutes to get my stuff—but it only took me five."

At the age of thirty-nine, she'd been married five times. This was scandalous behavior in her day, but she didn't care. Most of her neighbors soon learned to respect and like her. She was kind and generous. She fell in love at least one more time. The man's name was Ed Lewis. He was well read and literate. Ed had a ranch near Josie's. She spent some time at his place, and he spent time with Josie at her cabin. It was a good match, and it was one of the few times in her life that she was really in love. Her daughter-in-law didn't approve of her life style and was vocal about it when Ed stayed for supper and breakfast. The relationship went on for a while, but Ed and Josie, both volatile, couldn't quite iron out all their differences. They broke off the relationship but stayed friends.

Josie was accused of illegal activities more than once over the years. To make ends meet, Josie bootlegged whiskey, although she wasn't much of a drinker. She also made a very fine apricot brandy. She was also accused of rustling cattle when she was sixty-two years old but was acquitted. She put on a dress, something she rarely wore, did up her hair, and went to town for the trial. A Mormon stake president defended her. She told the court to look at her. "I'm a grandma," she said. "Do I look like I could rustle cows?" Little did they know! Never mind the cowhides with questionable brands that were found on her land. She argued that she was framed by people wanting to steal her ranch.

Like her sister, she had visits from former Wild Bunch members after the turn of the century. Butch saw her several times, as did Elza Lay. It wouldn't be surprising if Matt Warner dropped in for coffee once in a while. When the sun started to hang over the red rocks on Cub Creek and the warm wind blew away the afternoon heat, her homestead must have reminded her of her childhood home in Brown's Hole. Perhaps she reflected on her long life and the colorful characters she had known. Josie managed to live on her beloved Cub Creek for fifty years. When she was well into her eighties and no longer able to take care of herself, caring friends and family moved her into a nearby city.

She died not long after, worn out by life and desperately

missing her home. Like her mother who had passed on some sixty years before, she was one with the land she loved and worked.

Josie Bassett Morris's home can still be found in Dinosaur National Monument outside of Vernal, Utah. Guests are invited to look into her cabin, walk about her chicken coop, wade across the creek she drank from, or walk in the fields she cleared and raised her stock in, while keeping an eye out for rattlesnakes and pictographs on the canyon walls.

SUGGESTED READING

Adams, Andy. *The Log of a Cowboy: The Narrative of the Old Trail Days*. Boston: Houghton Mifflin, 2002.

Armstrong, Erma. "Aunt Ada and the Outlaws: The Story of C. L. Maxwell." *The Outlaw Trail* (winter 1997).

Baker, Pearl. *The Wild Bunch at Robbers Roost*. New York: Abelard-Schuman, 1971; reprint, Lincoln: University of Nebraska Press, 1989.

————. *Robber's Roost Recollections*. Utah State University Press, 1976.

Betenson, Bill (William). "Lula Parker Betenson." *The Outlaw Trail Journal* (winter 1995).

Betenson, Lula, and Dora Flack. *Butch Cassidy, My Brother*. Provo, Utah: Brigham Young University Press, 1975.

Briehan, Carl W. *Wild Women of the West*. New American Library, 1982.

Brier, Warren. "Tilting Skirts and Hurdy-Gurdies: A Commentary on Gold Camp Women." *Montana, The Magazine of Western History* (autumn, 1969).

Brown, Dee. *The American West*. New York: Charles Scribner's Sons, 1994.

Buck, Daniel, and Anne Meadows. *Digging Up Butch and Sundance*, rev. ed. Lincoln, Nebr.: Bison Books, 1996.

———. "Etta Place: A Most Wanted Woman." *The Journal of the Western Outlaw-Lawmen Historical Association* 3, no. 1, (spring-summer 1993).

———. "Etta Place: Wild Bunch Mystery Lady." *The English Westerners' Society Tally Sheet* (spring 1993).

———. "Showdown at San Vincente." *True West*, February 1993.

———. "Where Lies Butch Cassidy? *Old West* (fall 1991).

Burroughs, John Rolfe. *Where the Old West Stayed Young.* New York: William Morrow and Company, 1962.

Burton, Doris Karren. "Charley Crouse's Robbers' Roost." *The Outlaw Trail Journal* (winter 1993).

Carlson, Chip. *Tom Horn: Blood on the Moon.* High Plains Press, 2001.

———. "The Tipton Train Robbery." *The Journal of the Western Outlaw-Lawmen Historical Association* (summer 1995).

Churchill, Richard. *The McCarthys.* Timberline Books, 1972.

Davidson, Art. *Sometimes Cassidy.* Salt Lake City: Hawkes Publishing, 1994.

DeJournette, Dick, and Jan DeJournette. *One Hundred Years of Brown's Park and Diamond Mountain*. Mansfield Printing, Inc., 1996.

Drago, Gail. *Etta Place: Her Life and Times with Butch Cassidy and the Sundance Kid*. Plano, Tex.: Republic of Texas Press, 1996.

Dullenty, Jim. *The Butch Cassidy Collection*. Hamilton, Mont: Rocky Mountain House Press, 1986.

———. "The Farm Boy Who Became a Member of Butch Cassidy's Wild Bunch." *Quarterly of the National Association and Center for Outlaw-Lawmen History* (winter 1986).

Ernst, Donna B. "Black Gold and the Wild Bunch." *Quarterly of the National Association and Center for Outlaw-Lawmen History* (March 1944).

———. "Friends of the Pinkertons." *Quarterly of the National Association and Center for Outlaw and Lawmen History* (June 1995).

———. *From Cowboy to Outlaw: The True Story of Will Carver*. Sonora, Tex.: Sutton County Historical Society, 1995.

———. "The Sundance Kid: Wyoming Cowboy." *The Journal of the Western Outlaw-Lawmen Historical Association* (spring 1992).

Feitz, Leland. *Meyers Avenue: A Quick History of Cripple Creek's Red-light District*. Little London Press, 1977.

Gray, Dorothy. *Women of the West*. Les Femmes, 1976.

Hampton, Wade. "Brigandage on Our Railroads." *The North American Review* (December 1893).

Hayden, Willard C. "Butch Cassidy and the Great Montpelier Bank Robbery." *Idaho Yesterdays* (spring 1971).

Hine, Robert V. *The American West*. New Haven: Yale University Press, 2000.

Horan, James. *The Wild Bunch*. Signet Books, 1958.

Kelly, Charles. *Outlaw Trail*. Charles Kelly, 1938.

Kelsey, Michael R. *Hiking and Exploring Utah's Henry Mountains and Robbers Roost*, Provo, Utah: Kelsey Publishing, 1990.

Kildare, Maurice. "Bear River Loot." *The Real West* (September 1968).

Kouris, Diana. *Romantic and Notorious History of Brown's Park*. Wolverine Gallery, 1988.

———. "The Lynching Calamity in Brown's Park." *True West* (September 1995).

Larson, T. A. *History of Wyoming*. Lincoln: University of Nebraska, 1965.

Lavender, David. *The Telluride Story*. Ridgeway, Colo.: Wayfinder Press, 1987.

McCarty, Tom. *Tom McCarty's Own Story*. Hamilton, Mont.: Rocky Mountain House Press, 1986.

McClure, Grace. *The Bassett Women*. Athens, Ohio: Swallow Press/Ohio University Press, 1985.

Meadows, Anne. *Digging Up Butch and Sundance*. New York: St. Martin's Press, 1994.

Morn, Frank. *The Eye That Never Sleeps: A History of the Pinkertons National Detective Agency*. Bloomington: Indiana University Press, 1982.

Patterson, Richard. *Butch Cassidy: A Biography*. University of Nebraska Press, 1998.

———. "Did the Sundance Kid Take Part in the Telluride Robbery?" *The Journal of Western Outlaw-Lawmen Historical Association* (summer 1994).

———. *Historical Atlas of the Outlaw West*. Boulder: Johnson Books, 1985.

———. *The Train Robbery Era: An Encyclopedic History*. Boulder: Pruett Publishing, 1991.

Pointer, Larry. *In Search of Butch Cassidy*. Norman: University of Oklahoma Press, 1977.

Redford, Robert. *The Outlaw Trail, a Journey through Time*. New York: Grosset & Dunlap, 1976.

Reiter, Joan Swallow. *The Old West: The Women*. Alexandria, Va.: Time Life Books, 1978.

Selcer, Richard F. *Hell's Half Acre: The Life and Legend of a Red-Light District*. Fort Worth: Texas Christian University Press, 1991.

Slatta, Richard W. "The Legendary Butch and Sundance." *The Mythical West: An Encyclopedia of Legend, Lore, and Popular Culture*. ABC-CLIO: 2001.

Stegner, Wallace. *Mormon Country*. New York: Hawthorne Books, 1942.

Walker, Herb. *Butch Cassidy*. Baxter Lane, 1975.

Warner, Matt (as told to Murray E. King). *The Last of the Bandit Riders*. New York: Bonanza Books, 1938; reprint, 1950.

Michael Rutter is a freelance writer who lives in Orem, Utah, with his wife, Shari. They have two charming children and a very spoiled cat. Michael is the author of more than forty books, including *Camping Made Easy*, *Basic Essentials Fly Fishing*, *Outlaw Tales of Utah*, *Fun with the Family in Utah*, and *Utah Off the Beaten Path* for The Globe Pequot Press. When he's not fly-fishing, traveling or doing historical research, he teaches English at Brigham Young University.

THE INSIDER'S SOURCE

With more than 540 West-related titles, we have the area covered. Whether you're looking for the path less traveled, a favorite place to eat, family-friendly fun, a breathtaking hike, or enchanting local attractions, our pages are filled with ideas to get you from one state to the next.

For a complete listing of all our titles, please visit our Web site at www.GlobePequot.com. The Globe Pequot Press is the largest publisher of local travel books in the United States and is a leading source for outdoor recreation guides.

FOR BOOKS TO THE WEST